Supervision Skills for the Service Industry

How to Do It

D. V. Tesone

Rosen School of Hospitality Management
University of Central Florida

PEARSON

Prentice Hall

Upper Saddle River, New Jersey 07458

Library of Congress Cataloging-in-Publication Data

Tesone, D. V. (Dana V.)
  Supervision skills for the service industry : how to do it / D. V. Tesone.
    p. cm
  Includes bibliographical references and index.
  ISBN 0-13-110095-5
  1. Service industries--Personnel management. 2. Supervision of employees. I. Title.

HD9980.5.T47 2005
658.3'02—dc22

2003068918

Editor-in-Chief: Stephen Helba
Executive Editor: Vernon R. Anthony
Executive Assistant: Nancy Kesterson
Editorial Assistant: Ann Brunner
Director of Manufacturing and Production:
Bruce Johnson
Managing Editor: Mary Carnis
Creative Director: Cheryl Asherman
Interior Design: Pine Tree Composition, Inc.
Manufacturing Buyer: Cathleen Petersen

Full-Service Project Management:
Ann Mohan,
  WordCrafters Editorial Services, Inc.
Senior Production Editor: Adele M. Kupchik
Senior Marketing Manager: Ryan DeGrote
Marketing Assistant: Elizabeth Farrell
Composition: Pine Tree Composition, Inc.
Printer/Binder: Phoenix Book Tech
Cover Design: Mary Siener
Cover Printer: Phoenix Book Tech

Photo credits:

Michael Dinges/Getty Images, Inc.-Artville LLC, pp. 1, 15, 25, 41, 69, 79, 89, 101, 143; Stewart Cohen/Index Stock Imagery, Inc., p. 3; Richard Pasley/Stock Boston, p. 9; Mark Gilbert/Index Stock Imagery, Inc., p. 20; Jeff Greenberg/PhotoEdit, pp. 29, 48; Stephen Simpson/Getty Images, Inc.-Taxi, p. 33; AP/Wide World Photos, p. 44; Eye Wire Collection/Getty Images-Eyewire, Inc., pp. 55, 128, 149; Best Western International, p. 59; Cindy Charles/PhotoEdit, p. 63; Ed Lallo/Getty Images, Inc.-Liaison, p. 73; David R. Frazier/David R. Frazier Photolibrary, Inc., p. 82; Jeff Greenberg/Omni-Photo Communications, Inc., p. 84; Ryan McVay/Getty Images, Inc.-Photodisc, p. 93; Vic Bider/PhotoEdit, p. 96; John Riley/Getty Images Inc.-Stone Allstock, p. 105; Peter Wilson/Dorling Kindersley Media Library, p. 109; Dennis Harms/Images.com/CORBIS, p. 115; Joshua Ets-Hokin/Getty Images, Inc.-Photodisc; p. 117; Getty Images, p. 123; Jack Hollingsworth/Getty Images, Ind.-Photodisc, p. 131; Rob Reichenfeld/Dorling Kindersley Media Library, p. 134; David de Lossy, Ghislain & Marie/Getty Images Inc.-Image Bank, p. 147; Richard Ward/Dorling Kindersley Media Library, Key Terms icon used in all chapters.

Pearson Education LTD.
Pearson Education Singapore, Pte. Ltd
Pearson Education, Canada, Ltd
Pearson Education–Japan
Pearson Education Australia PTY, Limited
Pearson Education North Asia Ltd
Pearson Educación de Mexico, S.A. de C.V.
Pearson Education Malaysia, Pte. Ltd

10 9 8 7 6 5 4 3 2 1
ISBN 0-13-110095-5

*To the memory
of Dr. Gerald R. "Jerry" Work—
friend, colleague, and
elegant hospitality/tourism educator.*

Contents

Preface

This book is a practical guide for managers and supervisors to effectively work with people. The book is designed to provide influencing skills to accomplish the objectives of the organization through the activities of others. Most individuals are promoted to management or supervisory positions based on excellent performance in some position. Often, the position did not require individuals to supervise the activities of others. When people find themselves in positions to supervise others, they realize that new skills in addition to those that already exist are necessary for success in that position. Newly appointed supervisors sometimes have the tendency to do the work themselves, as opposed to delegating tasks. This is because the new supervisor is usually an expert at tasks for which others are now responsible. The fact is that the job of supervisors is to accomplish tasks and activities through the actions of other people. The good news for the new supervisor is that in performing most of the tasks personally, she may be sure they are done correctly. The bad news, however, is that she is not really performing the job of supervision.

The progressive positions in business organizations usually involve assuming responsibility for the actions of other people. That is what management is all about. Therefore, the manager who enjoys a developing career ends up in positions of responsibility for more people with each promotion. While management skills are important for career growth, these skills are not always taught to managers. This book is designed to provide the practicing supervisor and the student of management with a quick and practical guide for the supervision of people. The goal of this book is to help managers work smarter, not harder.

SUGGESTIONS FOR THE READER

This book consists of 12 chapters, arranged within three parts. The chapters in Part One of the book focus on conceptual (knowledge) skills required for effective supervision. Part Two contains chapters addressing practical (applied) skills for supervisors to use on the job. Part Three shows the reader job search strategies and how to actually be a supervisor in a live scenario. At the end of each chapter there is a short quiz for readers to test their knowledge of supervision. It is recommended that the reader reflect on actual scenarios in the workplace or do classroom role-play while reading this book. If this book is being used as part of a supervisory skills college course or workplace training program, the facilitator may encourage discussions of actual events to bring the topic to life. The reader is encouraged to convert the knowledge from this book into actual skills to be applied in the workplace. This may be accomplished through two activities. First, apply the knowledge immediately.

Turning knowledge into skills requires practice. Practice the knowledge within 24 to 48 hours after reading it. Second, teach these concepts to someone else. We learn through teaching. As one presents this new information to another person, one will reinforce the knowledge and be better prepared to use the knowledge in the workplace. Like the first suggestion, this technique should also be applied within 24 to 48 hours after reading and discussing the information.

ACKNOWLEDGMENTS

Sincere appreciation is offered to the reviewers of this book, whose valuable input contributed to its completion: Stephen E. Carlomusto, Johnson and Wales University; Carol Kizer, Columbus State Community College; Lindy Robinson, Johnson County Community College; and Diane Sinkinson, Cape Fear Community College.

Dana V. Tesone

CHAPTER ONE

Development of a Service Perspective

OBJECTIVES

At the end of this chapter, readers will be able to:

1. Understand the relationships of customers, supervisors, and other stake-holder groups from a service-oriented perspective.

2. Identify the components of the productivity model as the basis of value-added supervision.

3. Recognize types of behaviors that contribute to service performance standards.

4. Understand the relationship between performance standards and actual performance behaviors.

5. Identify the tools that are required for effective service supervision.

In the Real World . . .

You are a server in an upscale restaurant. You have a party of three, a dad, mom and their 6-year-old daughter. After serving the drink order, you ask to take the orders for appetizers and entrees. The little girl interrupts you and says, "Sir, my birthday is in two days and I would like a special treat. I was wondering if you have my favorite flavor of ice cream, butter pecan." You smile at her and say, "Well, we don't have that flavor, but I'll tell you what . . . while you are eating your dinner, I'll go in the back and make you some. I know how to make the best butter pecan ice cream you ever had. Would you like that?"

Needless to say, the little girl is ecstatic. You take the orders, return to the kitchen, and hand a dishwashing attendant $6. You tell him, "Run across to the convenience store and buy me a pint of butter pecan ice cream . . . and by the way, keep the change." (To be continued)

There are aspects of supervision that are generic to all business enterprises, including those within the domain of the hospitality and tourism industry. The supervision model taught in most business colleges focuses on the manufacturing paradigm, which involves the production of goods starting with resource procurement and ending with output and distribution of finished products. While this paradigm has partial applications to the hospitality and tourism industry, the crucial determinant of success in this industry involves service interactions with guests, passengers, clients, and customers.

This chapter presents an overview of supervision from the perspective of a service paradigm. It demonstrates the differences between practicing supervision in a factory or retail setting versus being a supervisor in a hotel, resort, restaurant, cruise company, or airline, as well as other enterprises encompassed within the hospitality and tourism industry. This chapter also provides a foundation of concepts that will be presented in detail throughout the book.

SERVICE INDUSTRY VERSUS MANUFACTURING/PRODUCTION INDUSTRY

Some individuals would have us believe that "the business of business is business, no matter what the business." This is not entirely true. There are two models in the business world, the manufacturing/production model and the service model.

The manufacturing/production model is pretty straightforward, with raw materials being converted into finished goods. Manufacturing managers do speak of "customer service"; however, their definition differs from that of managers in the service industry. To the manufacturing/production firm, customer service is all about the distribution of material products to an end-user, or buyer, who is called the customer. With this model, the salesperson promises the product to the buyer. The production personnel distribute the finished product through the supply chain to the customer. The customer service manager then handles complaints about defective or undesired products and processes those claims.

Take a full-service retail establishment, for instance. The customer enters the store, inspects the products offered for sale, listens to the advice of a salesperson, makes a selection, and takes the product home. In the event of product dissatisfaction, or the desire to return the product, the customer is directed to the "customer service department" to handle the return. Another example would include a nonretail scenario, in which a sales representative discusses the merits of a product and promises delivery to the customer upon the completion of the sales transaction. The product arrives at the customer's location. Should the customer find fault with the product, or wish to exchange the product, she is directed by phone or email to the customer service center to process that transaction.

The manufacturing/production model of business places emphasis on the production and distribution of tangible products to a customer. Once the customer receives the product, the transaction is considered to be complete. Should the customer require additional assistance after the sale, he is directed to another department within the company to handle exceptions to the standard sales transaction. In this model, the primary focus is on tangible products, with secondary focus on distribution and customer satisfaction. The opposite is true for a company in the service industry.

In a service industry company, the primary focus is on service to the customer, with secondary emphasis being placed on the production of tangible products. Practitioners in this industry range from highly professional service providers (health care, accounting, legal) to those who perform lesser skill-level functions (sanitation, landscaping, repairs, personal care). In the service business the *product is the customer*, so to speak; that is to say, the outcome of a service business provides more for a customer than a new computer, car, refrigerator, or package of chewing gum. A person is at least temporarily changed mentally or physically as a result of interactions with service providers. Some providers give customers peace of mind by handling complicated details such as financial and legal affairs. Personal-care providers alter the physical appearance of their customers. Leisure providers deliver luxury,

rest, and relaxation to rejuvenate their customers. Entertainment and event providers bestow "magical" moments and memories upon their customers. Lodging providers give traveling customers the comforts and safety of home. Epicurean providers give their customers delicious meals in relaxing social settings. Design providers produce individualized clothing or environments for their customers. And so on . . .

Since service is the product in the service industry, all successful firms are masters in the fine art of providing services. The same could be true for manufacturing/production businesses such as automobile dealerships, technology companies, and the like. However, most managers of these businesses appear to be satisfied with managing from a manufacturing/production mindset. What practitioners in the service industry know, that others may have not figured out, is that customer relationships are built and maintained through a company's commitment to customer service.

THE HOSPITALITY INDUSTRY

While all service enterprises focus on service as the main product, the epitome of a service operation falls within the domain of the hospitality industry. The hospitality industry includes services in the areas of lodging, food service, travel, tourism, recreation, entertainment, personal health and fitness, social events, meetings, and conventions. As we will learn later in the chapter, the complexity of these services is quite high in both intimacy and duration levels relative to the interaction with the customer (who is referred to as a "guest") in this industry. While the information in this book prepares all service industry personnel to practice effective supervision, the examples presented in it are taken from the hospitality industry. This is because a person with the ability to supervise in this industry is capable of effective supervision in any industry of choice.

COMMITMENT TO SERVICE

Stakeholders— Constituency groups of an organization (customers, employees, shareholders, and the community).

Internal customers— Workers within an organization who use the products and services of other workers to interact with external customers.

External customers— Those individuals who choose to purchase products and services from an organization.

Workers in any industry are famous for slogans and campaigns claiming quality service. The focus is usually on customer service. Very little emphasis seems to be placed on services provided to members of other **stakeholder** groups (shareholders, employees, the community). Interestingly, some hospitality/tourism organizations that claim high levels of customer service provide the exact opposite to their employees. Managers in some firms say they focus on the worker as an "**internal customer**."[1] Closer inspection of these companies often reveals unrealistically limited resources, antiquated systems, and stagnating bureaucracy. In fact, one of the incentives for promotion in some organizations is the opportunity to escape the customer by dwelling in an office and managing reports. Reports and forms, while necessary to some degree, serve as diversions from the "business of the business," which is to provide service to internal and **external customers**.[2]

In some cases reports and forms are used to feed an already bloated corporate bureaucracy that is upheld by senior-level managers. As the bureaucracy grows, the business becomes inverted, focusing inward toward the senior management group and away from the customers and other stakeholders. Because these organizations are out of touch with the stakeholder groups, they are reactive to changes in the external environment (factors outside the organization). This is contrary to the **proactive approach** of healthier competitors. Fortunately, this scenario is becoming more and more the exception to the rule . . . or is it? You decide the answer based on your own customer service and work-related experiences.

Proactive approach— Strategic thinking used to prevent problems from occurring.

WHAT IS SERVICE?

If someone were to ask the question, What is service? the manager's initial answer would be to say, "**It depends . . . .**" In this case it would depend on the nature of the industry providing the service. Most businesses focus on the distribution of products to customers. So, in manufacturing, wholesale sales, and retail sales, customer service is ensuring product delivery to the customer and handling any problems that may arise with the performance of the product. This is not the case in the services sector of business. In this sector, the physical product is really a byproduct of the services being rendered. For instance, in a quick-service restaurant (QSR) the product is the meal provided. The service consists of those interactions that occur between the customer and members of the staff from the time of entry to the restaurant through the time of departure from the restaurant. Hence, service consists of interactions that result in relationships among customers and staff members. Thus the term "customer relations."

"It depends . . ."— A standard response from one worker to another in an organization to indicate that the situation or environment is the determining influence on making optimal decisions.

Customer relationships may be measured by two factors. The first is the **intimacy level** or the intensity of the interactions. For instance, a QSR or retail worker merely takes the order and packages the product, so the intimacy with the customer is limited. On the other hand, a physician or a luxury hotel operator must know every detail about the client to provide the expected levels of service; thus a high level of intimacy exists with the customer during these interactions.

Intimacy level— The level of personal interaction with a customer in the process of providing products and services.

HOSPITALITY TIPS & CLIPS *Want a Successful Career? Live by These Rules*

- Always think like your customer.
- Build on a sound foundation. Pay your dues through education or the school of hard knocks.
- Always deliver a positive experience to your customers.
- Join professional associations, and keep learning by attending seminars and trade shows.
- Make friends with your competitors and others in your community who can serve as mentors.

- Look to those who went before you, and then combine their old ways with some of your new ways.
- Never forget the power of advertising, promotion, surveying, and researching as you try to improve your business.

Source: "Want a Successful Career? Live by These Rules." *Hospitality News* 1, no. 1: p. 4. Courtesy of *Hospitality News.*

Duration—The length of interactive time spent with customers in an organization.

The second factor used to measure the level of customer service is **duration** of time spent with the customer. The customer spends a few minutes with the QSR or retail worker, while he spends 30 minutes or so with a physician or a tax accountant; he spends hours in an airplane or full-service restaurant, and perhaps days in a luxury hotel. Figure 1.1 demonstrates examples of customer interactions in terms of intimacy and duration.

SERVICE VERSUS SERVITUDE

One term used to describe the services provided by leaders is *stewardship*.[3] Stewardship describes the intrinsic duty of leaders to provide services to their followers every day without being asked for assistance. They do this because they are truly concerned with the welfare of those individuals with whom they interact. In the hospitality/tourism industry we are trained to anticipate the needs of our guests (customers) and proactively act to satisfy those needs.[4] We don't do this because we "have to" do it; we do it because we personally and professionally enjoy the challenge of creating memorable experiences for our guests. That is why we hire new people for "attitude" in our industry. We seek those individuals who genuinely like people enough to engage in providing them with intimate levels of service for long durations of time. These individuals possess the security within their being that makes the difference between making a professional choice to serve others and having an insecure attitude of being in a position of servitude, in which they feel they "have to" serve others. The difference is a mental paradigm of personal security versus personal insecurity. The insecure individuals will move toward bureaucratic positions that are mostly self-serving as they pursue their careers.

Think for a moment about the great leaders in history throughout the world. Without exception, they all practiced "servant leadership,"[5] regardless of their specific calling. Now think about those not-so-great names in history.

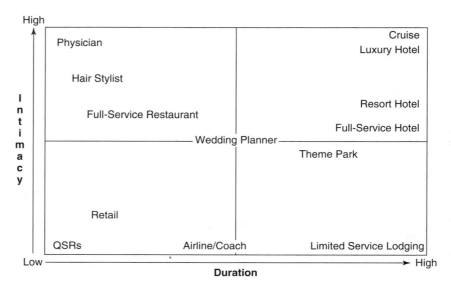

Figure 1–1. Customer service relationship model.

Were they individuals who provided services primarily for the benefit of others, or just themselves? Those who choose to provide service to others have chosen the highest path to self-fulfillment. They join the ranks of the likes of Buddha, Tao, Christ, Gandhi, Mohammad, Abraham, Socrates, and others. Consider the status of current-day professions: The physician provides service by healing sick people; the teacher is a servant of knowledge; the architect creates aesthetic structures for people's enjoyment while ensuring their safety; and so on. A path of service is a choice we make, while one of servitude is forced upon us.

THE ROLE OF THE SERVICE SUPERVISOR

We have discovered that service consists of interactions that create relationships with customers (both internal and external). So, what is the role of the service supervisor? At first glance it would appear that these individuals ensure positive interactions that result in positive customer relationships. But how do they do that? To answer this, we must consider the nature of supervision and management.

Supervision is the first level of management that oversees the work being performed by **line** and **staff workers**. As a person moves up the management ladder she spends less time supervising the performance of others and more time engaged in planning and organizing activities. Figure 1.2 depicts the levels of management and activities at each level.

Managers and supervisors are primarily responsible for achieving the objectives of the organization through the activities of others. So, what is an objective? An *objective* is a target for performance. It is something you want to accomplish for yourself, a department, or an organization. The **mission** or overall goal (the same as an objective) for a hospitality/tourism organization is "the acquisition and maintenance of guests."[6] In other words, every worker in the organization wants to keep the guests they have coming back, while taking steps to acquire new guests to add to the overall pool of guests who frequent the establishment. In the process of accomplishing this mission, supervisors and managers add **value** to the organization every day by enhancing **productivity**. Figure 1.3 describes a model for productivity.

The left side of the productivity model is called **input** and consists of human resources, material resources, and investment dollars for the

Line worker—A worker who interacts directly with customers and/or generates revenue for an organization.

Staff worker—A worker who advises or supports a line worker in an organization.

Mission—The philosophy that explains the purpose of existence of an organization.

Value-added supervision—Supervisory practices that enhance productivity.

Productivity—Adding value to the organization through reducing costs of resources and enhancing the quantity and quality of outputs.

Input—The supply of resources infused into a transformation process to yield outputs.

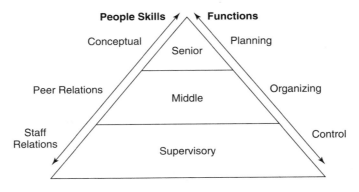

Figure 1–2. Management hierarchy.

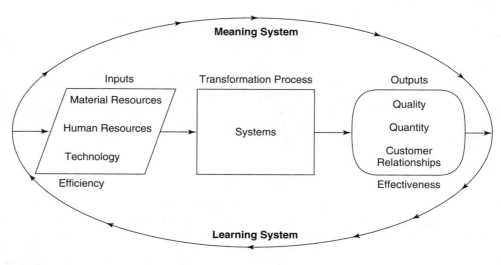

Figure 1–3. Productivity model.

The sidebar glossary on the left:

Transformation process—A process that converts resources (inputs) into products and services (outputs).

Output—The products and services produced within an organization.

Feedback—The process of reinforcing awareness of an interactive activity.

Learning—The process of enacting permanent change within an individual.

Meaning — Performance drivers that include mission, vision, philosophy, values, and beliefs of people within an organization.

Organizational culture—Shared values, attitudes, and beliefs among workers in an organization.

Objectives—Targets for performance (same as goals).

Strategies—Action steps implemented to accomplish objectives.

organization. The inputs flow into a system called the **transformation process** that converts (transforms) the resources into **outputs**, which are services and products for the guests. The bottom **feedback** loop is called the **learning** loop because it gives the organization information on how well it is performing and how to improve the system. The top feedback loop is called the **meaning** loop because it provides a comparison of actual performance of the mission and the **organizational culture** of the business and its workers.

To enhance productivity, supervisors and managers must find ways to reduce the cost of resources (inputs) and enhance customer services and products (outputs). Usually, the answers to productivity enhancement lie within the transformation process (systems). Since productivity enhancement contributes to the value of the organization, those who make that happen are called value-added workers.

So, supervisors and managers have three primary goals:

1. Practice the organization's mission.
2. Accomplish the organization's objectives through the activities of others.
3. Become a value-added supervisor by enhancing productivity every day.

If this is "what" managers and supervisors do, the next step is to explain "how" they do it.

STRATEGIES AND TACTICS

The mission and **objectives** for the hospitality/tourism organization are executed through action steps designed to reach the targeted goals (mission and objectives). Broad-range action steps are called **strategies**, which are mostly practiced by senior- and middle-level managers in the company. Supervisors are responsible for executing these strategies on a daily, weekly, monthly, and annual basis through narrow action steps called *tactics*.

Policies—Broad guidelines for performance in an organization.

Standards—The expectations for performance in an organization.

Procedures—Listing of tasks that result in meeting standards for performance.

Performance assessment—A comparison of actual performance to standards for performance (same as performance evaluation).

Strategies evolve into corporate **policies**, which are broad guidelines for performance throughout the organization. Supervisors convert these policies into **standards** for performance and **procedures**, which are daily action steps used by all staff members to meet the standards. For each performance standard, there is a list of procedures that are followed by the workers to meet that standard. The next step is for the supervisor to compile standard operating procedure (SOP) documents for the department and job lists for each position in the department that specify each standard for performance and the procedures for meeting each standard. Finally, the supervisor observes the staff members to ensure that actual performance is consistent with the standards and procedures for the operation.

This process is called **performance assessment** or evaluation, which compares actual performance with standards and procedures for performance. Figure 1.4 demonstrates the relationship of objectives, strategies, policies, standards, procedures, and performance assessment.

THE SUPERVISOR'S TOOLBOX

So far, it has been established that supervisors practice the corporate mission, achieve objectives, and enhance productivity by ensuring the practice of procedures designed to meet the standards for performance in the department. The next step is to describe the tools used by supervisors to influence staff members to make these things happen. Supervisors rely on a set of tools that provide the skills used in the practice of supervision. These influencing skills are essential for the practice of successful supervision. Each of the supervisory tools is described in detail throughout the text.

Perhaps the most important tool for supervisors is the ability to effectively communicate with workers, peers, and other managers. Communication involves active listening, verbal and written expression skills, and the interpretation

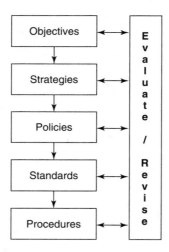

Figure 1–4. Performance assessment.

of nonverbal cues. One example of communication is the establishment of standards and procedures; another is job lists to guide worker performance.

Supervisors must be adept at identifying and resolving conflicts in the workplace. It is the job of the supervisor to maintain a work environment that is fair, uniform, and consistent for the workers. The ability to handle staff member complaints and grievances is essential to maintaining a healthy work environment.

Also, managers must establish leadership roles with the staff members concerning every aspect of job performance. For this reason, supervisors must possess solid skills in the areas of coaching, counseling, and discipline. These techniques are required for effective motivation, training, teambuilding, and leadership in the workplace.

SUMMARY

This chapter began with a service perspective that supports the old adage, "To give is to receive," which transitioned into a discussion of servant leadership, the highest calling for those of us engaged in services management. Next, we discussed the role of supervisors in our industry, which included information on strategies and tactics, as well as value-added supervision through productivity enhancement. Upon completion of our talk on the "whats" of supervision, we moved into a description of supervisory "hows" through a presentation of the influencing skills in the supervisor's toolbox.

WIFM—An acronym that stands for "What's in it for me?" used to describe the awareness of motivational factors for training and leadership.

Prior to our journey to develop supervisory skills, it would be appropriate to answer the **WIFM** (What's in it for me?) question.

Just as the supervisor starts a training program for staff members with WIFM, readers of this text should be presented with the personal and professional benefits associated with learning supervisory skills. The remaining chapters in this part address this issue in terms of career development, leadership development, and motivation awareness to facilitate the personal transformation of current and future supervisors.

. . . In the Real World (Continued)

As the family is finishing their entrees, you begin to prepare your "special" dessert for the little girl. You scoop the ice cream into a footed parfait bowl, add toasted almond sprinkles delicately over the scoop, and top it with a generous whipped cream cap, complete with a maraschino cherry placed on top of your "masterpiece." You place the parfait bowl on a doily-lined four-inch plate along with a demitasse spoon so your little guest may savor each dab of the ice cream treat. Next, you find the biggest chocolate-dipped strawberry available and place this strategically on the liner (this is mom's treat, since she is too diet-conscious to order her own dessert).

As the entrée plates are cleared you ask the little girl if she is ready for your special ice cream treat—after all, you have been slaving away in the back to make your special blend! You offer your plate presentation and ask the girl if she might want to give her strawberry to mommy.

While the little girl indulges in the best-tasting ice cream she ever ate and mom partakes of her oversized berry, you plug in $12 on the "open food" key, which adds nicely to your check total. Also, you can be sure that mom is reminding dad to treat you very well when he pays the bill.

You have just created "magic" for this family of three. You profiled the group and noticed that the key was to make mom happy. You chose to do this by doing some magic at her little girl's request. The little girl is happy, mom is happy (which makes dad happy), your sales total on the check is $12 higher, which makes the restaurant happy, and your 30 percent gratuity is calculated on that total, which should make you happy. Don't forget the dishwashing attendant, who is happy with the change he received from his trip across the street.

This is the service imperative or "magic," as those of us in hospitality like to call it. You have created a memorable experience for a few people, with very little effort on your part. This is what makes you a "value-added worker."

QUESTIONS FOR DISCUSSION

1. Consider the "In the Real World" example from the standpoint of a supervisor. Would you encourage this type of customer service among all the service staff? Why? Would this example enhance productivity in your restaurant? How? Imagine if all your servers performed this way. Would you be increasing productivity every day? Why?

2. It has been said that we "hire for attitude" in the service industry. What does this mean? What attitude are we looking for? How do we screen for it?

3. If the role of an employee is to provide excellent customer service, what is the role of the supervisor? Who does the supervisor serve? How does the supervisor do this?

4. Value-added supervisors enhance productivity every day. Does this mean they sacrifice service levels to save expenses? Does it mean they spend money freely and just increase the prices for their customers? If they don't do either of these things, what do they do to enhance productivity?

5. Being an effective supervisor requires developing certain skills. What are the required skills?

MINI-CASE

You are a supervisor in the transportation department of a major theme park. The department director has called all the managers and supervisors together for a brainstorming session on how to enhance productivity. Some people recommend slashing costs as the answer, while others suggest revenue increases only. Still others focus on streamlining transformation processes as the sole answer.

After hours of discussion the director steps up to address your group. She says, "Guys, productivity is a balancing act." She draws the productivity model on a flipchart. She says, "You have to consider both sides when enhancing productivity, which means if you take action on the right side, you must take action on the left side." She continues, "For right now, let's forget about the middle. That will come in handy when we decide how to fix both the left and right sides of our model." She concludes, "As I see it, there are only three ways to do this, although if you are really creative, there may be a fourth one that will work."

Question:

What are the three or four things?

Hint:

It has something to do with increases, decreases, and maintaining levels on each side of the model.

KEY TERMS

Duration	Line worker	Policies	Standards
External customers	Meaning	Proactive approach	Strategies
Feedback	Mission	Procedures	Transformation process
Input	Objectives	Productivity	Value-added supervision
Internal customers	Organizational culture	Staff worker	WIFM
Intimacy level	Output	Stakeholders	
It depends . . .	Performance assessment/ evaluation		
Learning			

CHAPTER QUIZ

1. Service consists of interactions that create customer relationships.   **T**   **F**
2. Inputs consist of resources.   **T**   **F**
3. Duration and intimacy levels help determine customer service strategies.   **T**   **F**
4. Stewardship is leadership service to the followers.   **T**   **F**

5. Communication skills are not part of the supervisor's
   toolbox.   **T**   **F**

6. WIFM is an important consideration in appealing to
   people's needs.   **T**   **F**

7. Value-added management has nothing to do with
   productivity.   **T**   **F**

8. Employees are not members of the stakeholders group.   **T**   **F**

9. It is possible to be an effective supervisor without having
   standards.   **T**   **F**

10. The mission includes the purpose of the organization's
    existence.   **T**   **F**

ENDNOTES

1. Brian Albrecht, "Professor Finds Faith along Rural Highways with Theme Parks
   and Sites Inspired by God," *The Plain Dealer* (Jan. 4, 2003): E.1.

2. Ibid.

3. Ramona M. Wis, "The Conductor As Servant-Leader," *Music Educators Journal*
   89, no. 2 (Nov. 2002): 17.

4. Greg Stafford, "Crisis Management and Recovery: How Washington, D.C., Hotels Responded to Terrorism," *Cornell Hotel and Restaurant Administration Quarterly* 43, no. 5 (Oct. 2002): 27.

5. Ibid.

6. Leonard L. Berry, "Understanding Service Convenience," *Journal of Marketing*
   66, no. 3 (July 2002): 1.

CHAPTER TWO

Career Development through Personal Transformation

OBJECTIVES

At the end of this chapter, readers will be able to:

1. Understand the concept of learning through experience and evolution.
2. Identify the stages in the work life development model.
3. Recognize the value of lifelong learning.
4. Understand the relationship of career development as part of the overall quality of life.

In the Real World . . .

You work at a hotel and are taking a coffee break in the employee cafeteria. The director of human resources sits down with you. His name is Danny and he is about 20 years older than you. After some chit-chat, you ask him how he got to where he is in his career. He sits back, gazes upward, and starts to tell his story.

"I came from a lower-middle-class, broken family," he begins. "I started working at a local hotel just to earn some extra money when I was 16, and by the time I was 17, I was working full-time. My goal was to get out of the house by the time I was 18, which I did. I took college courses, but was more interested in making money. By the time I was 20, I had worked in just about every hotel job there was. Then, I was promoted to management and learned how to work with people as a supervisor through the "trial and error" method, which was not always fun. However, I was lucky enough to have plenty of mentors who showed me how to be a better manager. I was really ambitious back then and got promoted to the next level of management every two years or so. I really worked hard and found that I enjoyed turning operations around and developing other workers."

He continues, "But then I got really burned out on operations management. I noticed that the human resources director seemed to have better working hours than the ops managers and spent most of her time helping the employees. Although I had lots of college credits, I didn't have a degree, which was a requirement for the job. So, I went back to school to get my degree in my off hours. Between school and work, I was really learning a lot about management at that time. Finally, after a few years, I got my degree and a job as the number 2 manager in the human resources department. By now, I was working on my master's degree on weekends; I was eventually promoted to human resources director."

"But don't you want to be a GM?" you ask. He says, "I thought I did back then, but when they offered me those promotions, I turned them down. You see, I am at a stage where I really love the work I do, even though I could make more money by going back into operations. I like helping people and I have the time to focus on other aspects of my personal development. I'm on a different journey these days than I was back in my achievement years. But I'll tell you this . . . I am a lot happier with my life than most of my friends."

The next thing you know, time has flown by and it's time to go back to work. As you do, you keep Danny's story in the back of your mind. (To be continued)

It has been said that we have a choice in life that will occur 20 years from now. We could end up with 20 years of experience, or one year of experience 20 times.[1] The difference lies in what we choose to do with our experiences. If we choose to learn and grow each year, we will be sure to eventually possess 20 years of experience; or we may choose to maintain the same mindset over the years. Neither choice is "right" or "wrong"; they are just choices available to us. However, it has been said that the definition of insanity is to repeat the same behaviors with the expectation for a different outcome.[2] Others claim upon reflection to have "failed their way to success."[3] And Aldous Huxley proclaims, "It is not what happens to you in this world, but instead what you do with it."[4] So, we have choices in this life. We could choose to remain the same as we are now, or we could choose to learn and grow every year. Some leaders recommend that we totally reinvent ourselves every year, which may be good advice given the nature of the dynamic environment that surrounds us.[5]

You may recall the "learning loop" presented in the last chapter. It describes the method for organizations to learn from their experiences. The same is true for individuals—we learn from our personal and professional experiences. In fact, one definition of learning is to enact permanent change in an individual.[6] Figure 2.1 provides a presentation of a model for learning and change.

If learning is the enactment of change, and we are changing from something we already are, that change must take us to a higher level in terms of our personal evolution through development. Hence, learning provides development. And reflection upon that development transforms us from who we were before the learning process to who we are after the learning process. Thus, we have participated in the process of personal and professional transformation, or permanent change. Those of us who choose paths of lifelong learning are engaged in continuous personal and professional transformation. One byproduct of this process is the path of career development.

THE WORK LIFE DEVELOPMENT MODEL

Just as we progress on a journey of biological maturity from birth through death, we also pursue a path of "work life" or career development. Figure 2.2 depicts the stages of work life development. Each stage in the model represents an escalated maturity plateau that is reached by some, but not all, workers seeking career progression.

Work Life Development Model—A model that depicts the developmental life cycle of an individual from the introduction to full-time work through retirement from full-time work.

Primary and secondary research, as well as anecdotal observation in hospitality organizations, has resulted in the construction of the **Work Life Development Model** for workers in these organizations.[7] The model is based on development theories of researchers to include Kohlberg,[8] Dewey,[9] Piaget,[10] Maslow,[11] Shea,[12] and Perkins-Reed.[13] The Work Life Development Model is based on the assumption that the mental, social, emotional, and spiritual development of the full-time worker is influenced to some degree by work experiences, just as these areas of personal development are partially shaped by childhood and adult living experiences. While most adults reach full biological

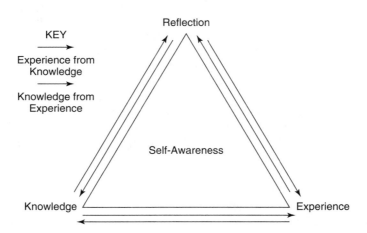

Figure 2–1. Learning process model.

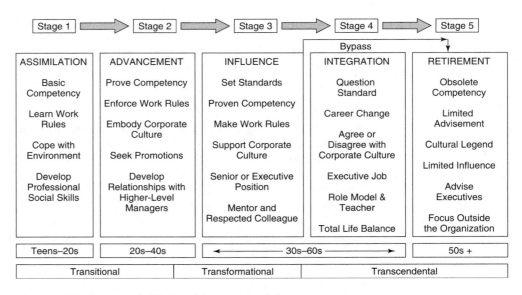

Figure 2–2. The work life development model.

maturity, this is not the case for everyone. The same is true for work life development. Most but not all workers reach at least four of the five stages.

THE FIVE STAGES OF DEVELOPMENT

Assimilation stage—
The first stage in the Work Life Development Model in which individuals become accustomed to performing in full-time positions with organizations.

There are five stages of development for workers in service-based organizations. The first stage is called the **Assimilation** stage.

New entrants to the workforce are members of this group. Workers in their late teens through middle 20s usually fall in this range. During Assimilation the worker possesses basic levels of competency. The worker often feels unsure concerning the direction of career progression. He is learning to assimilate work with other aspects of life. The worker is in the process of learning the rules and policies in the workplace, as well as coping with the corporate environment. In this stage, workers often move laterally to other positions inside an organization or with other organizations to gain different experiences. Also, they begin to develop social skills with peers and supervisors.

Advancement stage—
The stage in the Work Life Development Model in which individuals are seeking higher-level positions of authority and responsibility.

A second stage of worker development is called the **Advancement** stage. Individuals at this level are often in their middle 20s to early 30s and have had 5 to 10 years of work experience or have a college degree and a few years of experience. These people are concerned with demonstrating work-related competency. Workers are usually in positions to enforce the work rules and possess a clear understanding of the corporate culture. Often, these workers have decided on a basic career path and have been promoted at least once to supervisory or management positions. At this stage there are usually strong peer affiliations with other managers and supervisors. Workers at this level are beginning to develop comfortable relations with senior-level managers.

The third stage of development is called the **Influence** stage. People become members of this group usually in their early to middle 30s, with most remaining at this stage into their 60s or the time of retirement from the organization. In this stage a person is recognized as being fully competent. She is

---

HOSPITALITY TIPS & CLIPS *Most Successful People . . .*

- Start from scratch.
- Become valuable to their bosses and become indispensable.
- Know how to be part of a team.
- Are able to find joy in others' successes.
- Strive to be great at what they do.
- Are always trying to learn more.
- Focus on the future.

- Look for solutions.
- Pay attention to the details.
- Don't blame others for problems.

Source: "Most Successful People. . . ." *Hospitality News* (October 2002): p. 32. Courtesy of *Hospitality News*.

Influence stage—The stage in the Work Life Development Model in which an individual is in a position to serve as a role model to others.

Integration stage—The stage in the Work Life Development Model in which an individual chooses to function in a state of values-based balance.

Critical shift—A major change in attitudes, values, and beliefs for an individual.

usually in a position to make the work rules and policies and is a symbol of the organization's cultural values. She is in a senior line or staff management position, usually at the director level. The individual is often involved in mentoring relationships with promising subordinates. Also, a strong level of collegial rapport is established with peers at this stage.

Some but not all of those in the Influence level will transition into the **Integration** stage.

The remaining individuals will move directly from the Influence stage into Retirement, the fifth and final stage of work life development. Members of the Integration stage almost identically resemble those at the upper end of the Influence level, with one exception. While the Influencer has transformed within the organization, the Integrator has transcended beyond a specific organization. Balance for the Influencer means doing whatever it takes to maintain the corporate position, regardless of time requirements and value conflicts. The Integrator, however, is in need of total life balance and is not willing to compromise personal values for professional position.

Sometimes an individual in the Influence stage will experience a **critical shift** from egoistic (status) principles to esoteric (self-fulfillment) principles. When this happens, the individual is entering the Integration stage of work life development. As a person makes this transition, a feeling of balance among all aspects of the self begins to emerge, and the individual now has the desire to perform professional work that provides balance or integration with the other components of self-awareness or identification.

The Integrator is highly energized as a result of the intrinsic meaning of his work. This person exhibits passion, self-mission, vision, and dedication to the work itself. He is highly motivated, yet not consumed with work. It is the nature of the work itself and the perception of the work by the individual that cause these characteristics to become evident. A person in this stage is relentless in the pursuit of meaningful contributions to others resulting from his work. He rises as an inspiring leader, mentor, teacher, cheerleader, and steward. The question that arises is whether the Integrator will do these things in his current organization or will pursue a career change. The answer depends on the congruence between the organizational culture and the need for the Integrator to perform self-fulfilling work.

How many people actually experience the Integration stage before they retire? The answer to this question is unknown. It is likely that a small

number of total workers reach this stage before retirement, with a larger number engaging in the experience during retirement. If there is any truth to the evolution of newer generations, we may expect larger numbers of people to reach the Integration stage at younger ages than those who came before.

Retirement stage— The stage in the Work Life Development Model in which individuals stop contributing to an organization after a long period of service.

The fifth and final stage of the Work Life Development Model is called **Retirement.** As stated previously, not all individuals experience every development stage, but all do eventually retire from the workplace. Retirement may be voluntary (the decision to stop working) or involuntary (the occurrence of traumatic disability or biological death) on the part of the worker. Some workers choose to "mentally" retire (stop being productive) before they physically retire (actually leave the workforce).

Some individuals never get past the Assimilation stage and retire after a career of chronic unemployment. Others get stuck in the Advancement stage; even though they have attained senior-level positions, they don't possess the ability to be a source of influence in the organization. Most individuals who reach the Influence stage of their work life wait until Retirement to pursue integrated activities. Preretirement individuals in the Integration stage usually choose to retire when their "work is done" and they have groomed a talented individual to replace them in the organization. For Integrators, retirement usually means a new form of personally meaningful work. While most individuals who advance in the Work Life Development Model cycle do hold senior-level corporate positions, this is not a requisite for moving into advanced stages. Any experienced hospitality worker can recall examples of highly developed people who choose to work in lower-level positions in the organizational hierarchy. As is the case with all aspects of life, appearances may very well be deceiving.

SUMMARY

This chapter has presented career development issues as demonstrated by the Work Life Development Model. When it comes to career development, there are no right/wrong, good/bad decisions. Therefore, one person can offer

HOSPITALITY TIPS & CLIPS *Beware! Don't Get Too Comfortable*

If you're too comfortable in your work, you could become obsolete. To make it in today's fast-paced world, you must keep learning and growing. How do you stretch your learning muscles? Here are a few suggestions:

- **Have a positive attitude.** If you don't have a good attitude about learning, you'll never get enough energy to get outside of your comfort zone, which is where most learning and opportunity exist. Successful people have a positive outlook about change and continuous improvement. Larry Curtis, CEO of Shari's Restaurants, always says he can't wait to learn something new from everybody he meets each day. What a wonderful outlook!
- **Look for learning opportunities.** Learning doesn't just happen. You have to consciously and actively seek to learn. There's room for improvement on almost anything we do at home or at work. Looking for ways to improve and learn from tasks keeps our minds open to learning. By attending trade shows and seminars and visiting frequently with others in your same line of work, you can learn a tremendous amount of practical information. One operator gets up an hour early every morning to read the latest business book. He tries to keep ahead of his competition by honing his business skills.
- **Experiment.** Make a conscious effort to try different things, be it driving a new route to the gym or trying a different process at work. It does not have to be a huge change; take a small step to get started. Remember that if you keep doing what you've been doing, you'll keep getting what you've been getting. This applies to many aspects of our work, including marketing, hiring, training, menu selection, purchasing, and so forth. Always be willing to try new options.
- **Make a list.** Write down a list of 50 abilities that, if you had them, would help you grow and learn. For example, consider improving your writing skills. It would not only make you a better communicator, but also might provide you the opportunity to write your own press releases. The ability to motivate is another good trait, whether it's for yourself or your employees. Pick a couple that you can do within 90 days and go for it. Go online and see what websites can help you. Attend a class. Go to your nearest bookstore and see what self-help books are available on the topics that you wish to improve. Work your way through the list.

Never get too comfortable and think you know it all. If you snooze, you lose.

Source: "Beware! Don't Get Too Comfortable." *Hospitality News* (November 2002): p. 11. Courtesy of *Hospitality News*.

another person very limited advice on the matter. One rule of thumb is for us to do the work we love at the salary we want to earn, in a location where we want to be. These things in addition to a path of lifelong learning will result in contentment, prosperity, and personal/professional growth. Some people aren't sure what they want to do for a career. One approach to overcoming this barrier is to eliminate those types of things we don't want to do until just a few things are left.

There is a parable about a man who climbed a mountain.[14] He put all his energy into pulling himself up the steep slope. With the last of his strength, he finally reached the top of the mountain. He stood there, feeling exhausted, and looked out at the scenery, only to find he had climbed the wrong mountain! Choose your own mountain. Don't climb mountains that someone else wants you to climb.

. . . In the Real World *(Continued)*

Danny's story has been in the back of your mind for a few hours. You finish your shift and are just about to exit through the employee area of the hotel. You decide to stop by the human resources office on your way out. Normally, Danny is swamped with conferences, but as luck would have it, he is just doing some work on the computer. You stop in and he invites you to sit down.

You tell him, "I've been thinking about you and it sounds like you have really 'paid your dues' and have changed a lot over the years. I have also been watching some other people, and some seem content, while others seem to be really stressed. I guess it takes a long time to figure out how to be happy in life."

He smiles at you and says, "I think it will happen a lot quicker for you than the older people you see around here." "Why?" you ask. He says, "I don't know. But over the years I have watched newer generations come and go, and it seems to me each one is a little more evolved than the last, certainly more evolved than my generation."

You ask, "How do you know this is true for me?" He smiles again and says, "I just know."

QUESTIONS FOR DISCUSSION

1. Discuss your goals for the next year, 2 years, 5 years. Are they written down? If not, do you think it would help if they were written down? Why or why not?

2. Think about people you know who are in school, at work, friends, relatives, whatever. Can you identify where they are in terms of the Work Life Development Model?

3. Do you know anyone who is unhappy with her or his career? Why do you think this is so? Do you know anyone who loves his or her job? Why is this so?

MINI-CASE

You have just been hired as a supervisor for a (fill in your business) company, and you are observing the performance of individuals in your work unit. You notice that your work group is quite diverse in terms of age, sex, national origin, religion, language skills, race, background, and experience. Each of the six workers in your unit is unique in one way or another, as are three senior-level managers. The following is a profile of these people from your observations:

· Fred is a nice guy who shows up for work about 10 minutes early for each shift and does a very nice job overall. On his last performance review he was asked to write down his goals for next year, and he stated that he intends to be a rock star.

· Cybil has been with the company for about a year and is a hard-driving individual who wants to work her way into management. She is clearly an overachiever who is very focused on her work.

· Jimmy is having a difficult time showing up on time for work. He often skateboards to work straight from the beach and smells like seaweed. As far as his absenteeism, you seem to notice a direct correlation between his missed shifts and the daily surf report.

- Joe is a middle-aged guy who does a great job and uses the money he earns at the company to fund his newly organized cult, which believes in alien gods among us that come and go by spaceship.
- Eddy is a good worker, but he seems to have problems getting along with his fellow workers. The supervisor has moved him into different work areas, and he seems to have interpersonal conflicts wherever he works. The supervisors like him, but the coworkers would like to kill him sometimes.
- Buffy is very popular with the guests and clientele. She is attractive and has a bubbly personality. She works for the company to help finance her dancing career.
- JoAnn is a senior-level manager who has been with the company for a number of years. She is a nurturer who sets a great example for other managers and mentors a few of the newly appointed supervisors. Most people think she will become the president of the company one day.
- Bill is a senior manager at the same level as JoAnn. He seems to do his job with ease and is a highly respected leader and mentor. He was offered the job of president but turned it down, saying "it wasn't worth the additional headaches." He has an almost "Zen" aura about him, with most of the staff respecting his level of wisdom.
- Stella is the company president. She is an avid golfer and boater and seems to always be on vacation. JoAnn and Bill really run the company. Stella is somewhat out of touch with modern management thinking, but she wants to maximize her 401(k) by continuing to collect her salary. JoAnn can't wait to take her place, and Bill couldn't care less about taking the president's job.

Based on the brief profiles of these people, identify which category they may be placed in on the Work Life Development Model, and explain your rationale. Keep in mind that a person could fall within early to late stages of the category. Then, for each individual, determine if they are in a transactional, transformational, or transcendental mode. This will influence the way you communicate with each of them.

KEY TERMS

Advancement stage	Critical shift	Integration stage	Work Life Develop-
Assimilation stage	Influence stage	Retirement stage	ment Model

CHAPTER QUIZ

1. Learning involves the enactment of change in a person.   **T**   **F**
2. Personal transformation has nothing to do with change.   **T**   **F**
3. We may or may not choose to learn from experiences.   **T**   **F**
4. There are four stages in the Work Life Development Model.   **T**   **F**
5. All people eventually assimilate to full-time work.   **T**   **F**
6. Stages of development may be reached without having a big job.   **T**   **F**
7. The only retired people are those who leave an organization.   **T**   **F**

8. Integrated people are focused on life-balance.   **T**   **F**

9. Personal transformation sometimes includes a critical shift.   **T**   **F**

10. While most people reach stages at certain times, age is not a factor.   **T**   **F**

ENDNOTES

1. John Waterbury, "Hate Your Policies, Love Your Institutions," *Foreign Affairs* 82, no. 1 (January–February 2003): 58.

2. S. E. Kruck, "Framework for Cognitive Skill Acquisition and Spreadsheet Training," *Journal of End User Computing* 15, no. 1 (January–March 2003): 20.

3. Ibid.

4. Michael Rogers, "Aldous Huxley: A Biography," *Library Journal* 127, no. 17 (Oct. 15, 2002): 99.

5. D. V. Tesone, *Tactical Strategies for Service Industry Management: How to Do It*, Boston: Pearson (2003).

6. David L. Luechauer, "Creating Empowered Learners: A Decade Trying to Practice What We Teach," *Organization Development Journal* 20, no. 2 (Fall 2002): 42.

7. Ibid.

8. Michael H. Morris, "The Ethical Context of Entrepreneurship: Proposing and Testing a Developmental Framework," *Journal of Business Ethics* 40, no. 4 (November 2002): 331.

9. Shelley A. Lee, "Rhetoric, Revisited," *Journal of Financial Planning* 15, no. 9 (September 2002): 17.

10. Adam Lefstein, "Thinking Power and Pedagogy Apart: Coping with Discipline in Progressivist School Reform," *Teachers College Record* 104, no. 8 (December 2002): 1627.

11. Steven J. Hanley, "Maslow and Relatedness: Creating an Interpersonal Model of Self-Actualization," *Journal of Humanistic Psychology* 42, no. 4 (Fall 2002): 37.

12. Anonymous, "Advice for Starting or Improving Your Mentoring Program," *Accounting Office Management & Administration Report* 1, no. 6 (June 2001): 11.

13. Holly L. Angelique, "Promoting Political Empowerment: Evaluation of an Intervention with University Students," *American Journal of Community Psychology* 30, no. 6 (December 2002): 815.

14. Henry J. Richards, "The Opening Chapters of Nelson Estupinan Bass's Last Novel, Al Norte de Dios *[Lucifer: The Other Son of God]*," *Afro-Hispanic Review* 22, no. 1 (Spring 2003): 78.

CHAPTER THREE

Leadership and the Supervision of Service

OBJECTIVES

At the end of this chapter, readers will be able to:

1. Understand the relationships of leaders, followers, and the environment (situation).

2. Identify the characteristics associated with leadership traits.

3. Recognize types of interactions that are associated with transactional leadership.

4. Understand the concepts of transformational and transcendental leadership.

In the Real World . . .

You work as a security officer at a large resort. Because of your classes at the university you work an overlapping shift between the day and early night shift. There is a security manager who supervises each shift. You work 4 hours with the Alpha shift manager (Brad) and 4 hours with the Beta shift manager (Sharon). Both managers are former police officers and are very proficient in safety and security procedures. The difference between these two individuals as managers, however, is like day and night (no pun intended).

Brad is a micro-manager who doesn't believe in employee empowerment. He commonly casts blame on the officers for their mistakes; but he is the first to take credit for the ideas of others. He is a stickler for policies and procedures, even when it seems there should be exceptions based on a set of circumstances. He tends to have "favorites" on his shift who receive preferential treatment over some of the other, harder-working officers. The officers don't complain about Brad to the director because Brad seems intimidating. Brad often berates the officers in front of their peers and the guests.

Sharon, on the other hand, is every bit as proficient as Brad in the technical aspects of security, but she is also respected as a leader among the officers on her shift. As a matter of fact, most of the officers in the department request transfers to her shift when there are open positions. She is considered to be firm but fair in her approach with the officers. She often takes the blame for things that go wrong, even if it was caused by one of her officers. She always listens to the staff for new ideas to improve performance and takes action to implement good ideas. She is quick to give credit to her officers for their contributions to the shift. She is always available to assist the officers, but lets them handle incidents and make decisions. She always coaches them in private after an incident that could have been handled better. Most of her officers are good performers, and she will go out of her way to take care of them.

As a matter of fact, that is how you ended up with your split shift. She knew you were a good performer and that you took morning classes at the university. She is the one who arranged your schedule to accommodate your school activities. (To be continued)

PRACTICAL ASPECTS OF LEADERSHIP

Leadership—The demonstrated ability to influence others to willingly participate in activities.

Leadership is a common topic of discussion in organizational and institutional settings. Curricula in schools of business administration and hospitality/tourism management include courses, seminars, or cross-curriculum infusion of topical areas that are related to leadership concepts. The word *leadership* is commonly used in the course of daily conversations in professional and administrative settings. Printed literature includes articles and advertisements for professional development workshops on the topic of leadership. Also, employers rank leadership skills toward the top of desired abilities of candidates for supervisory employment. Finally, a good deal of academic research has been conducted to develop leadership paradigms.

While the concept of leadership is much discussed, it still remains difficult to describe. Individuals seem hard-pressed to provide agreeable descriptions of what leadership really is. This factor may contribute to the many definitions that have been provided to describe the many aspects of leadership.

WHAT THE RESEARCHERS SAY ABOUT LEADERSHIP

Machiavelli—Author of *The Prince*, who suggested that leaders are born, not made.

The old **Machiavellian** belief that leaders are born, not made, remains present in modern-day thought among certain individuals. Others contend that leadership may be learned by anyone with a desire to lead others. If this is true, the question for trainers and educators seems to be, "How do we teach people to become leaders?"

One study provides comparisons between leadership and management in organizations to determine differences between the activities of leaders versus managers.[1] Another investigation discusses characteristics and qualities of leaders as means to provide case study examples of leadership situations.[2] One researcher provides a developmental model as a means for teaching leadership relations.[3] Some studies identify leadership credibility factors as determined by the perceptions of others to describe leadership qualities.[4] Other academic investigators take research-based model approaches to present paradigms to develop an understanding of leadership phenomena.[5] Finally, recent research provides focus on the transformational leadership paradigm to describe leadership dimensions,[6] as well as universal systems models.[7]

Interdependent state—A mental state of balanced interactivity of give-and-take, in which an individual or subsystem is not controlled by nor isolated from a system.

It would seem that regardless of the approach taken to understand and teach leadership, three **interdependent** factors must be considered. First, we must observe the behaviors and attempt to identify the characteristics of leaders. Second, we should gain an understanding of the perspectives of followers. Third, we must analyze contributions of the environment or **situation** to leader/follower interactions. This view may seem simplistic; however, when attempting to understand complex concepts, simplification may be the means through which we clarify our understanding.

Situation—The environment in an organization at a given time.

It is apparent that those who have been mentored or exposed to dealing with great leaders possess a clear snapshot of leadership in action. Therefore, it may be possible that an experiential approach to learning is appropriate in the study of leadership topics.

LEADERSHIP AND MANAGEMENT

People often confuse leadership and management, when in fact they are two different concepts. One illustration of this is the advice for supervisors to manage "things" and lead "people." This suggests that leadership is an influencing activity while other aspects of management refer to planning, organizing, and controlling functions.[8] It is important to note that not all managers are leaders and not all leaders are managers. Think for a moment about people with supervisor titles that just don't come across to you as leaders. Now, consider those with no formal authority who seem to influence coworkers to follow their lead.

Stewardship—Willing service to ensure the welfare of constituents.

Some experts speak of leadership from the standpoint of the support role owed to the followers, which is referred to as "**stewardship**" qualities of leaders.[9] Ancient philosopher Lao Tzu proclaimed that leaders must learn to follow, which is one of the signs of stewardship.[10] One tendency of effective leaders is their willingness to share the role of leader and follower in appropriate situations. Leaders also demonstrate the capacity to provide simplified interpretations of complex issues.[11]

HOSPITALITY TIPS & CLIPS *Are You a Manager or a Leader?*

There are many managers and only a few true leaders. Here are the skills that define the elite group of men and women we call leaders.

Effective leaders have the ability to:

- **Build or use a compelling vision** of what's achievable and then communicate that vision to others.
- **Encourage people,** sharing authority and responsibility in order to make others feel significant and needed.

- **Establish objectives** that make the most of opportunities and resources, and make plans to reach those objectives.
- **Think creatively.** Find untapped opportunities, look for additional options, locate new needs, and solve problems.

Source: "Are You a Manager or a Leader?" *Hospitality News* (August 2002): p. 30. Courtesy of *Hospitality News.*

EXAMINING TRADITIONAL MODELS AND THEORIES OF LEADERSHIP

There are plenty of traditional models and theories concerning the topic of leadership. Review of traditional models by the experts seems to provide evidence that research is not the key to developing a practical understanding of leadership. A number of research articles are available for review. Yet, the data provide ineffective knowledge for the purpose of imparting leadership skills. This, once again, seems to provide evidence that the concept of leadership is phenomenal in nature.

Organizational theory frames provide us with categories of leadership strengths. However, no single frame provides a holistic picture of an actual leader. Instead, leaders are categorized as having conceptual strengths in structure, relations, political skills, or facilitative skills. Most widely acclaimed leaders possess strengths in all these categories.

Trait leadership—A theory of leadership that suggests that the characteristics of an individual determine the ability to lead others.

A number of studies have been conducted to identify characteristic and response theories to explain leadership.[12] **Trait leadership theories** cite personal characteristics, which help us determine to what extent leaders will gravitate toward transactional versus transformational leadership styles.

Behavioral theories focus on internally motivating factors of task and relations, while contingency theory considers the same tendencies from external motivating aspects. These traditional theories assume an objective viewpoint of interactions between leaders and followers. Other research departs from this tradition by identifying means used by leaders to elicit follower participation. These are basically focused on communication skills. The underlying inference is that leaders manipulate followers through symbolic gestures such as rites and rituals, or that leaders create mythical perceptions in the minds of the followers. Regardless of the focus, the technique seems to involve the construct of perceived realities consistent with the beliefs, attitudes, and values of the followers.

In actual practice, it may be true that leaders possess and employ the ability to communicate in terms identifiable with followers' cultural systems.

Empathy—Personal identification with the emotions felt by another individual.

This activity might be viewed as the ability of the leader to **empathetically** communicate with followers through an innate understanding of the internal value systems of individuals and groups. While this may be labeled as a form of manipulation, it may be more accurately described as effective managerial communication to achieve common and constructive outcomes.

ETHICS AND LEADERSHIP

Is there a moral component in the leadership paradigm? An interesting departure from the traditional viewpoint associated with the achievement of transformational leadership through power and influence is the diminished moral connotation within the model. Some of the research indicates that the moral aspect has evolved into a code word for innovative and motivational leadership. It would be hard to imagine a true leader who did not create an image of personal morality in the minds of her followers. Even leaders in illicit environments portray a code of personal values in their behaviors and communications.

Regardless of the semantics, most researchers and practitioners agree that credibility is the key to a leader's ability to influence others. This credibility evolves from perceptions of the leader by peers, followers, and other leaders. Credibility is attained by people's perceptions of a person's behavior and expression of thoughts. The leader, by nature of his relationship to others, is highly scrutinized in this regard. Therefore, it seems likely that the credibility factor is greatly influenced by the moral and ethical value systems of the person occupying a leadership position.

Finally, discussions concerning leadership diversity provide a departure from traditional views presented by other authors. In this case the word *traditional* refers to the white male leader, as opposed to the nontraditional

leader of different gender or color (to include national origin). While it is certainly true that cultures have provided limitations to the achievement of legitimate power possessed by repressed classes of people, it is unlikely that differences exist as to the inherent ability of these individuals to lead. It appears that these writings are concerned more with cultural challenges as opposed to actual leadership concerns.

EMERGING THEORIES AND MODELS

Change agentry—The activity of implementing methodical change strategies.

Emerging theories in leadership reflect the dynamic environment in which organizations and institutions currently function. Less focus is placed on narrow models of leadership. Holistic leadership paradigms are now emerging. Visionary aspects of leadership are becoming a dominant consideration in discussions of leadership effectiveness. **Change agentry** is also a prominent concern. It stands to reason that today's leaders need to be skilled visionaries capable of enacting change. Organizations are rethinking, restructuring, and revitalizing the types of work that are done and processes aimed at the achievement of outcomes. Therefore, it is appropriate for effective leaders to possess skills in supporting the followership in these environments.

The leader of today deals with such diversity as to require much more advanced levels of sophistication than former leaders. Emphasis in emerging leadership models provides focus on the dynamics of the followership. Individuals in today's organizations possess stronger values of individualism and sophisticated convictions with regard to quality of lifestyle issues. Also, today's workforce is comprised of individuals who are knowledgeable and adamant in the preservation of individual rights in the workplace. This impacts the ability of leaders to provide effective influence over others and further enhances the moral component of leadership influence.

PURPOSE, MISSION, AND VISION

Certain environments provide what one might call "motivating missions."[13] In such cases, people seem to be naturally motivated to perform at peak levels. Usually, these scenarios are project based. Common examples would be special events that occur in organizations that challenge and energize workers to work toward a common purpose and to achieve a common set of goals. During these events, the job of leadership is somewhat simplified. Also, during these times, unsuspecting leaders tend to temporarily emerge. The unfortunate aspect of this scenario is that it seems to be unsustainable. That is, it is temporary and when the inspiring mission is fulfilled, the performance levels and enthusiasm seem to drop to "normal" (sometimes mediocre) levels.

The challenge for leaders is to provide sustainable purpose and mission that motivate the workforce. The reason this is challenging is that most institutions and organizations do not serve a naturally glamorous or exciting purpose. Therefore, it becomes the challenge of the leader to embrace and communicate the mission and purpose in ways that impassion others.

The current trend in organizations and institutions goes beyond purpose and mission to include vision statements. Unfortunately, when the word *statement* is added, the bureaucrats become licensed to turn visioning into a paper and pencil (disk and keyboard, these days) exercise. One expert draws contrasts and comparisons to approaches taken by managers versus leaders to develop and communicate visions.[14] The managers have a tendency to formulate administrative representations, similar to what is taught in strategic planning sessions. The leaders bring the vision to life. They depict the vision in terms that are consistent with the value systems and description preferences of the people in the organization. In essence, leaders bring visionary concepts to life.

BUILDING AND SHARING POWER

According to some researchers, leaders possess the ability to use informal means to align people.[15] They do this by developing informal networks within various areas of the organization. Bureaucratic managers rely more on formal lines of communications such as written reports and job descriptions. These formal documents do have their place in an organization or institution. However, bureaucrats rely more heavily on these tools than do their leader counterparts.

Leaders are usually highly skilled communicators. Whether these skills are acquired or inherent, the leader recognizes the power behind effective communications. They use all means of communication available to them. Their mannerisms, body language, appearance, posture, and examples are orchestrated to drive home the message being sent to people. Leaders also possess the ability to convert complex concepts into simplified strings of messages. This probably is attributable to a thorough understanding and

---

HOSPITALITY TIPS & CLIPS *Who's Left in Charge? Pick Middle Management Wisely*

Nothing undermines an organization like poor middle management. The greatest oversight by any employer is to allow poor supervisors to become dictators over the staff. If productivity is down and morale is low, the cause may be in who you left in charge. Here are a few common problems with managers who are really "manglers" instead of managers.

- Inconsistent changes in procedures caused by managers making personal decisions that do not always support company policy

- Favoritism
- Poorly delivered instructions, training, and requests such that employees aren't sure what is expected
- Big egos—supervisors wanting all the glory to themselves
- Discrimination and sexism

Source: "Who's Left in Charge? Pick Middle Management Wisely." *Hospitality News* (August 2002): p. 10. Courtesy of *Hospitality News*.

rapport with people in the organization. Finally, leaders recognize the importance of active listening. They realize that by listening effectively, they can better understand the people with whom they are dealing. Leaders are keenly aware of the importance of information gained through informal interactions.

SELF-ANALYSIS AND CONTEXTUAL RELATIONS

More than one person has proclaimed that prior to leading, one must learn to follow. In the same way, before one can know others, she must know herself. This may be the basis of the understanding of human behavior that many leaders seem to possess. Leaders take time for introspection and creative thinking. Popular phrases for this activity might be meditation or focused reflection. No matter what the format or title, it is believable that leaders spend a good deal of time in contemplative silence (daydreaming might be another label for this activity). It is possible that this quiet time permits an individual to analyze the self and interactions with others. This activity may help to create a certain type of wisdom within an individual. Sometimes we call these people "sage."

One expert reminds us that leaders see individuals as holistic beings.[16] People are more than their positions, accomplishments, and status. They are fully developed human entities with all of the experience, knowledge, and emotions possessed by the human race. Leaders take the time to consider the human factors of people. They are also capable of identifying individual talents, preferences, motivational factors, and feelings. The researchers also remind organizations to be on the lookout for corporate entropy.[17] In organizations, there are signs that indicate the settling-in of bureaucratic thought processes. As these processes take hold, the organization begins to decline. One sign is when individuals begin to lose sight of the purpose, mission, and vision of the organization. These symptoms, if left unaddressed, may lead to cultural shifts in organizations in which leadership values may ultimately decline, only to be replaced by bureaucratic values, which may be detrimental to the survival of those corporations.

DEVELOPING AND IMPROVING LEADER RELATIONS

Leaders are often self-developing people. Also, as people who self-analyze, leaders are usually aware of their strengths and areas for improvement. Someone once said that great leaders have great weaknesses.[18] This may be true. Regardless, leaders appear to be aware of those areas in which they need assistance. For this reason, the leader would have a tendency to enlist the support of individuals who may assist him in specifically required areas. Leaders also have a tendency to appropriately empower or align with others to facilitate accomplishment of the overall mission. In this sense, leaders are sensible. They seem to recognize that none of us is as good or smart as all of us.

In addition to possessing an awareness to select human capital to increase overall strengths, leaders often have the ability to energize individuals toward achievement. It is likely that they do this in a manner that provides

personal satisfaction to people as well as benefit to the organization or institution. Therefore, leaders maximize relations with others for the common welfare of all.

TRANSACTIONAL AND TRANSFORMATIONAL LEADERSHIP

Transactional leadership—
A theory of leadership that focuses on the interactions of the leader and followers to determine leadership effectiveness.

Transactional leaders are those who possess the ability to influence others through highly developed interpersonal relationship skills. The power of influence is certainly a key skill shared among all leaders. Leaders may rely more heavily on this set of skills depending on the specific organizational structure. Often, in these organizations individuals are provided legitimate power through the attainment of positions, such as division or department director. However, in some settings workers may tend to resist people who have been given titles. One factor that may contribute to these types of attitudes may be the tendency by senior managers to appoint individuals who do not possess credibility with the workers to positions of power and influence. Thus, lack of credibility may usurp acceptance of formal authority. However, people who possess appropriate levels of credibility with the workers in these organizations seem to be unaffected by the overall lack of respect for people with formal job titles.

THE NATURE OF CHANGE

For years now, students of management have been told about the impact of external environmental factors on organizations. Models are provided to assist managers with identifying and predicting external events, for the purpose of making decisions to limit threats and opportunities looming outside the

HOSPITALITY TIPS & CLIPS *Things to Learn to Become an Effective Manager*

Great managers aren't born—they are developed. Put into practice the following principles and techniques. You will become a more effective and successful manager. Learn how to:

- Improve your decision-making and problem-solving skills.
- Communicate effectively, one on one and in groups.
- Motivate your employees to do their best.
- Become a leader, not a prodder.
- Market yourself to your boss, and get promoted faster.
- Manage your time to reach your goals.

- Stimulate creativity and innovation in yourself and in those around you.
- Manage stress.
- Plan to succeed with any project.
- Build a productive organization, one that can be counted on to get the job done right.
- Advance your career by changing jobs when an opportunity comes your way.

Source: "Things to Learn to Become an Effective Manager." *Hospitality News* (June–July 2002): p. 33. Courtesy of *Hospitality News.*

organization. Being good students of management, they have learned to perform auditing, scanning, forecasting, and analytical activities. A factor that seems to be overlooked is the importance of making decisions to modify how the organization operates to remain congruent with its environment. At the same time, we are entering an era in which those external factors of influence are becoming more dynamic at exponential proportions. As the world around us changes, people must also change. For this to happen, people must accept responsibility and accountability for changing their lives. Evolutionary change involves personal growth. Leaders who pursue paths of personal growth for themselves and their followers are practicing the highest level of interaction called **transformational leadership.** In today's business environment both transactional and transformational leaders are considered to be change agents.

Transformational leadership—A theory of leadership that considers value systems of followers, leaders, and organizations as components of the leadership process.

CHANGE AGENTRY

Most of us have met individuals who are natural troubleshooters. These individuals are always seeking challenges that require implementing change. Some personality tests identify people who prefer to work in troubleshooting capacities. Troubleshooters who possess training and skills in effective change implementation may be referred to as *change agents.*

This is not to say all change agents are troubleshooters. In the same sense, not all troubleshooters are effective change agents. Some are muck stirrers. While they mean well, they lack the ability to systematically implement change that is accepted by others. An organizational aspect that change agents and troubleshooters undoubtedly face is **conflict.** As a matter of fact,

Conflict—Differences of ideology demonstrated through interactive behaviors.

most of us deal with conflict on a regular basis. We have a tendency to consider conflict to be negative. However, there are forms of conflict in organizations that are constructive. This type of conflict may be called *managed conflict*. A leader who recognizes the synergistic outcomes of creative idea generation might welcome this form of conflict. When constructive conflict is present, the threat of "groupthink" is reduced. This type of conflict fosters multiple viewpoints to generate outcomes greater than those that may be established by a single individual working alone.

SUMMARY

In this chapter we have identified the characteristics of leaders. Interactions among leaders, followers, and a given situation (environment) are the basis of transactional leadership. Transformational leadership considers these same factors in addition to the evolutionary growth of all participants in the interactions. This type of influence among individuals requires perceived credibility on the part of leaders; thus leaders are viewed as possessing qualities associated with personal and professional integrity. Transformation is preceded by the enactment of change. Leaders are change agents who systematically develop individuals to grow with the dynamic external environment. While the topic of leadership has been widely considered in research settings, the best way for practitioners to become skilled leaders is to model and engage in mentorship relationships with those established leaders in the workplace.

... In the Real World (Continued)

A number of months have passed and you are being considered for a promotion to the position of security supervisor. In this job, you will assist one of the shift managers. The reason you are up for this promotion is based on your great performance as a security officer. As you can imagine, Brad gave you a moderate recommendation for the promotion because you were not one of his favorites. Sharon stated an excellent case on why you deserve the promotion to security supervisor.

You are now interviewing for the promotion with the current security supervisor and she comments that you probably learned most of your leadership skills from Sharon. You reply, "Actually, I learned quite a bit from Brad as well." The security supervisor looks puzzled. You explain, "I learned a lot about what to do from Sharon and a lot about what not to do from Brad."

QUESTIONS FOR DISCUSSION

1. Some people say that leadership is a natural ability, and others say that these skills may be learned by anyone who wants to be a leader. What do you think?

2. If you analyzed your leadership style and came to the conclusion that you are mostly task oriented (focused on what needs to be accomplished), what style would you look for in your assistant? Would he be just like you or different? Why?

3. Think about great leaders in history or in your personal experience. What qualities do you think made them so great?

4. Now, consider those leaders who may not be classified as good leaders at all. Where were they deficient? Is there anything to be learned from their examples?

MINI-CASE

You have just been hired as a supervisor for a security department at a large resort. You notice that the staff appears to be lax, with many of them failing to meet standards for performance. During your assessment of the work unit you learn that former supervisors were somewhat apathetic and failed to provide solid supervisory techniques such as communicating standards for performance and training new staff. Now you have inherited a group of individuals who are unfamiliar with the standards and have never been trained. While you really can't blame them for their substandard performance, you must turn this work unit around. This will require firmly communicated and enforced standards for performance and retraining of the existing staff.

Question:

What will be your leadership style during this intervention? Will you act as a transactional leader or a transformational leader?

Hint:

Is it too soon to use one of these, given the nature of this situation?

 ## KEY TERMS

Change agentry	Leadership	Trait leadership	Transformational
Conflict	Machiavelli	Transactional	leadership
Empathy	Situation	leadership	
Interdependent	Stewardship		
state			

CHAPTER QUIZ

1. Leaders are born, not made.   **T**   **F**
2. Credibility is a major factor in leadership effectiveness.   **T**   **F**
3. Everyone wants to be a leader, so only the strong ones get to
   lead.   **T**   **F**
4. Trait leadership theories consider leadership characteristics.   **T**   **F**
5. All leaders are appointed by the organization.   **T**   **F**
6. The right way to lead depends on the situation at hand.   **T**   **F**

7. Strong leaders operate in a mental state of interdependency.   **T**   **F**

8. Good leaders rely on the power of their appointed positions.   **T**   **F**

9. Transactional leadership focuses on interactions with
    followers.   **T**   **F**

10. Stewardship leadership focuses on the welfare of the
    followers.   **T**   **F**

ENDNOTES

1. Staff, "Management and Leadership Should Not Be Confused," *ENR* 249, no. 23 (Dec. 2, 2002): 76.

2. David A. Whetten, "A Social Actor Conception of Organizational Identity and Its Implications for the Study of Organizational Reputation," *Business and Society* 41, no. 4 (December 2002): 393.

3. John F. Mahon, "Corporate Reputation: A Research Agenda Using Strategy and Stakeholder Literature," *Business and Society* 41, no. 4 (December 2002): 415.

4. Erich N. Brockmann, "Tacit Knowledge and Strategic Decision Making," *Group and Organization Management* 27, no. 4 (December 2002): 436.

5. Ibid.

6. Robert J. Alban-Metcalfe, "The Transformation Leadership Questionnaire (TLQ-LGV): A Convergent and Discriminant Validation Study," *Leadership & Organization Development Journal* 21, no. 6 (2000): 280.

7. John Quay, "Leadership and the New Science: Discovering Order in a Chaotic World, 2nd Edition," *Consulting to Management* 13, no. 2 (June 2002): 59.

8. Littleton M. Maxwell, "The Challenge of Front-Line Management: Flattened Organizations in the New Economy," *Personnel Psychology* 55, no. 1 (Spring 2002): 244.

9. Gerald F. Cavanagh, "Virtue as a Benchmark for Spirituality in Business," *Journal of Business Ethics* 38, no. 1/2 (June 2002): 109.

10. Therese F. Yaeger, "Leading OD through Linkage: Meet Dr. Phil Harkins," *Organization Development Journal* 20, no. 1 (Spring 2002): 53.

11. Ibid.

12. Adrianna Kezar, "Expanding Notions of Leadership to Capture Pluralistic Voices: Positionality Theory in Practice," *Journal of College Student Development* 43, no. 4 (July/August 2002): 558.

13. Gene A. Brewer, "Why Elephants Gallop: Assessing and Predicting Organizational Performance in Federal Agencies," *Journal of Public Administration Research and Theory* 10, no. 4 (October 2002): 685.

14. Ibid.

15. Ibid.

16. Ibid.

17. Ibid.

18. Anne D. Smith, "From Process Data to Publication: A Personal Sensemaking," *Journal of Management Inquiry* 11, no. 4 (December 2002): 383.

CHAPTER FOUR
Employee Motivation

OBJECTIVES

At the end of this chapter, readers will be able to:

1. Identify a few theories of employee motivation.
2. Apply motivational strategies to managing workers.
3. Recognize differences in individual motivators.
4. Apply techniques to motivate groups.

In the Real World . . .

You are a supervisor for the kitchen stewarding department at a large hotel. You run the early evening shift. You took the shift over about a year ago. Ever since you started, the performance levels keep getting better, employee turnover is down, and people from other departments want to work on your shift. Your staff is very culturally diverse and everyone respects each other. The chief steward is your direct supervisor and is very impressed with the way you run your shift.

During a recent performance appraisal interview, the chief was commenting on how much your staff respects your leadership ability. He said off-handedly, "How do you do it? You have so many individuals from various backgrounds, the work is terribly difficult, and yet they all seem to get along and will set the world on fire for you." You said to him, "It is really just a matter of understanding what motivates people to do good work. For example," you continued, "take this guy, he works two jobs and is going to vocational school. The most important thing for him is to have time to juggle these activities. So, I work with him when it comes to the schedule. And Sheila over there, she has been dumped on her whole life. All she wants is a little respect, so we all refer to her as 'Ms. Sheila' and she loves it. This is in stark contrast to that guy over there. He is basically shy and when he isn't working, he produces great paintings. I don't make a fuss over him; instead I look at pictures of his latest productions and comment on them. Heck, I even bought one of his paintings."

The chief was impressed with your understanding of human motivation. He said, "You know, I hate to tell you this 'cause I wouldn't want to lose you. But the housekeeping director approached me to see if it is okay if she recruits you as an area manager. This will be a promotion for you, and I couldn't blame you if you decide to talk with her about the opportunity." You answered, "Thanks, John. Some bosses would have tried to keep a guy like me from getting promoted just to make their lives easier. I respect you for that." (To be continued)

Motivation—
The willingness that creates intentions for behavior among individuals and groups.

Motivation may be defined as a willingness to do something. Managers are interested in motivation applications because they want workers to be willing to perform tasks and activities aimed at accomplishment of the objectives of the organization.[1] Workers who are willing to do the work do better jobs. Willing workers also permit the manager to act as leader instead of manager. Motivated people do not need to be managed. They simply require leadership to remain focused on the collective attainment of objectives.[2]

WHAT MOTIVATES PEOPLE?

Various factors motivate individuals in different ways. This is because motivation is based on the perception of unfulfilled wants, needs, and desires.[3] These perceptions vary among individuals. For instance, most people agree that money is a motivator. The experts indicate that, for most people, it isn't the money that motivates, but the unfulfilled material needs associated with having money.[4] Some people are definitely motivated by the opportunity to earn unlimited incomes. These people have a tendency to work in commissioned sales positions. Other people value earning the most income in the shortest period of time spent working. These people have a tendency to work

---

HOSPITALITY TIPS & CLIPS *Attention Managers: Here's What Most Employees Want*

1. Treat them as a partner, respect and involve them, and share information.
2. Provide them with important challenges in their careers.
3. Value their contributions.
4. Let them know what they do is appreciated.
5. Use their suggestions and ideas and give them credit.
6. Demonstrate a caring attitude. Be fair and stand by them when something happens, such as a personal crisis.

7. Hold them accountable for what they commit to and let them know that they are a necessary part of a team.
8. Pay them fairly and appropriately.

Source: "Attention Managers: Here's What Most Employees Want." *Hospitality News* (November 2002): p. 7. Courtesy of *Hospitality News*.

---

for gratuities or large bonuses. Another group of people prefer to work in pleasant surroundings with specifically scheduled work hours and standard work routines. These people may prefer administrative positions. Managers are often motivated by challenging work, achievement, recognition, and a personal sense of accomplishment as an important member of an organization. Managers usually perceive the need to make a decent income but often choose management positions over more lucrative positions such as commissioned sales jobs. For many managers, a performance bonus is primarily a measurement of accomplishment, with the actual dollar amount representing the reward for achievement.

Individuals have varying needs and priorities of need. For this reason, there is no general rule concerning motivators for different people. The manager does not possess the ability to motivate another person. This is because motivation comes from within a person, not from external sources. Therefore, the best a manager can do is to get others to motivate themselves. Managers accomplish this by identifying unfulfilled perceived needs and wants for each individual. Once needs and wants are identified, the manager makes every attempt to combine need fulfillment with performance outcomes. This combination results in motivated workers.

Money as a Motivator

For most workers, money is not an effective motivator. Instead, it is a potential dissatisfier.[5] This may be partially due to compensation structures in organizations; most people are paid for time worked. Organizations have limited resources concerning the amount of money that can be paid to workers. When a worker receives a pay raise, that person is content for a few weeks. After that time period, the amount of the paycheck becomes the expectation and the worker feels that more money is deserved. However, there are ways to structure compensation practices to attach financial rewards to performance achievements. In these cases, money (or at least its intrinsic meaning to the worker) can serve as a strong motivator.

Theories of Motivation

Over the years, many researchers have developed theories concerning motivation of individuals and groups of people. This chapter presents a few popular concepts. The theories that describe the "whys" of human motivation are referred to as content theories. Those that explain "how" to motivate people are considered to be process theories. In this section we start with content theories and conclude with process theories of motivation.

CONTENT THEORIES

Hierarchy of needs theory—A content theory of motivation that suggests a scale of individual needs from lowest to highest.

Hierarchy of Needs Theory

Psychologist Abraham Maslow developed a model, called the **hierarchy of needs theory,** that depicts unfulfilled wants and needs as motivating factors.[6] Maslow contends that five categories of needs exist in a hierarchy that ranges from lower-level needs to higher-order needs. As one set of needs becomes mostly fulfilled, the set of needs on the next level becomes motivators. Maslow indicates that individuals who mostly fulfill lower-level and higher-order needs will seek fulfillment of the highest possible need. That need is called the need of self-actualization. Self-actualization occurs when a person seeks to be all that a person can be in a holistic sense. This person is at peace with self, having attained a self-perceived level of spiritual, material, and

personal contentment. In the past, most people began to pursue self-actualizing needs in later adult years. However, current generations of adults start reaching for self-actualizing goals in their early 20s due to higher levels of evolution among newer generations.[7] According to Maslow, less than 2 percent of the world's population attains the level of being completely self-actualized. The hierarchy of needs is presented in Figure 4.1.

Two-Factor Theory

Researcher Frederick Herzberg agrees with Maslow that there is a hierarchy of lower- to higher-order needs (a **two-factor theory**). Herzberg suggests that the lower-order needs are extrinsically (externally) based, while the higher-order needs are intrinsic (internal).[8] According to Herzberg, lower-order needs are not motivators; rather, they are hygiene factors. By this, Herzberg implies that lower-level needs need to be satisfied for individuals to pursue higher-order needs.

> **Two-factor theory—** A content theory of motivation that defines external needs as hygiene factors and internal needs as motivators.

The potential satisfaction of the lower-level needs does not motivate people to perform work. Instead, the absence of needs fulfillment, such as pay, working conditions, and safety, will make workers dissatisfied. Dissatisfied workers will not be motivated by higher-order needs. Maslow and Herzberg provide two of the most popular content theories of motivation. A comparison of Herzberg's theory to Maslow's theory is presented in Figure 4.2.

PROCESS THEORIES

Process theories of motivation describe how people respond to motivators through behavior. While the content theories described previously discuss the "whys" of human behavior, process theories focus on "how" to motivate workers to enhance their performance levels.

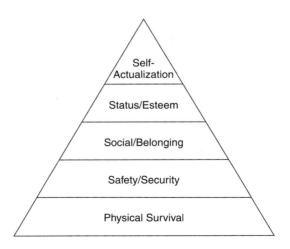

Figure 4–1.

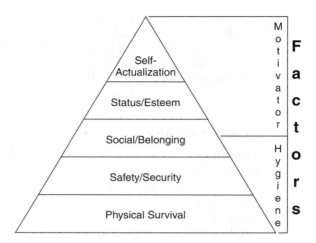

Figure 4–2.

Behavioral Modification Theory

The behavioral school of thought focuses on reinforcement and punishment associated with stimulus and response to explain motivation. Behaviorist B. F. Skinner provides a model of reinforcement of desired behaviors as a form of motivation.[9] Reinforcement occurs in response to a desired behavior. For instance, praise for a job well done will reinforce future positive performance. Those who subscribe to this reinforcement philosophy believe that only positive actions should receive a response; punishment does not provide a sustainable change in a person's behavior or attitude. Therefore, some individuals contend that undesirable behavior should be ignored. This theory is called *extinction*. However, as discussed in former chapters, managers are responsible for addressing all incidents of performance-related behavior. Therefore, managers must provide reinforcement for desired behaviors and other appropriate responses for undesired behavior. It is important to remember that workers, unlike pigeons, are cognitively and emotionally developed individuals.

Reinforcement always rewards desired behaviors. It does this in two ways. **Positive reinforcement** attaches something pleasant to the performance of desired behaviors. **Negative reinforcement** takes away something considered to be unpleasant as a reward for desired behavior. For instance, a worker does a particularly good job on a project. A nice bonus would be positive reinforcement; removing an unpleasant task (like side-work for a restaurant server) would be negative reinforcement. Both are approaches to providing rewards for desired behaviors. Therefore, negative reinforcement is not a bad thing; it is just another way of providing a reward.

Other Process Theories

While behavioral modification is perhaps the most widely used process motivational tool for supervisors, there are other theories that are relevant to managers above the supervisory ranks. One is called the **expectancy theory,**

Behavioral modification theory—A process theory of motivation based on a system of behaviors and consequences that contain stimulus and response relationships, in the forms of reinforcing desired behaviors and punishing negative behaviors.

Positive reinforcement—Initiating a pleasant experience as a reward for desired behavior.

Negative reinforcement—Removing an unpleasant experience as a reward for desired behavior.

Expectancy theory—A process theory of motivation based on the perceived value and probability of attaining a reward for performance.

HOSPITALITY TIPS & CLIPS *Management Tips for Motivation*

- There's nothing that can substitute for making the employee feel valued. Verbal praise, respect, treating employees like customers were all common responses.
- Bonuses in the form of cash, bottles of wine, and gift certificates seem to work well for managers. A number of managers said they trade coupons for dinners at their restaurants with other businesses in the area for items such as movie passes, car washes, a free night's stay for hotels, and even dinners at other area restaurants.
- Recognitions such as Employee of the Month with a special parking place and a day off with pay were described as effective incentives.

- Free food and drinks for each shift worked was another common response.
- To create a sense of fun and excitement, a number of managers stated that they hold contests for upselling where employees can earn gift certificates and cash.
- Finally, one manager said that having a regular schedule for salary and wage increases really helps to retain employees.

Source: "*Hospitality News* Readers Respond with Management Tips." *Hospitality News* (June–July 2001): p. 19. Courtesy of *Hospitality News*.

---

which deals with structuring rewards that hold value relative to the amount of energy expended by the worker to earn the reward; this is coupled with the expectation that the reward will actually be received by the worker upon achieving the stated goal.[10] For instance, the supervisor may be empowered to award a $50 bonus to the restaurant server with the highest amount of wine sales. If this is worth the upselling effort to the server and if the server

---

HOSPITALITY TIPS & CLIPS *Employee Incentives*

It's amazing what incentives can do to increase job productivity and satisfaction. Here are a few simple, low-cost incentives that might be worth a try.

- Give certificates for car washes.
- Give a certificate for lunch in the boss's office. The boss will serve the employee lunch.
- When an entire team achieves a goal, hire a massage therapist to come and give massages to employees.
- Give a certificate that entitles the employee to come in 2 hours late one day. (This should probably be prearranged.)

- Cash! Everyone loves cash. It doesn't have to be big amounts.
- A thank-you note telling your employee why you appreciate his or her efforts is sometimes worth more than a prize.
- Movie passes to a local theater are always a hit.
- Gift certificates to a local bookstore or record store will make your employees happy.

Source: "Employee Incentives." *Hospitality News* (March 2001): p. 14. Courtesy of *Hospitality News*.

trusts that the bonus will be paid at the end of the shift, this may result in additional wine sales.

Equity theory—A process theory of motivation based on the perception of fairness among individuals in a work unit or organization.

Management by objectives— Top/down and bottom/up goal-setting that are planning and performance evaluation tools used in participative organizations.

Another process theory that is relevant to compensation practices is the **equity theory**.[11] This concept is based on perceived fairness in pay and benefits among the workers in a department. Individuals who believe they are paid less than others performing similar work are likely to lose motivation to perform. Managers should keep this in mind when designing compensation structures.

One powerful motivational tool is shared goal-setting from the top of the organization down through every level. This technique is called **management by objectives** (MBO).[12] In organizations that do not implement this strategy, supervisors may choose to provide it at the departmental level. They do this by establishing department goals and sharing those with the workers. Based on these goals, each worker contributes with her objectives for performance. Supervisors and workers agree on these goals and use them to evaluate performance. The advantage to this process is that workers feel a sense of "buy-in" to the objectives for the department. This generates a sense of ownership and empowerment on the part of each worker. When we "own" a goal, we usually strive to make it happen.

OTHER FACTORS THAT CONTRIBUTE TO MOTIVATION

Motivation concepts are certainly important for understanding the dynamics of workers' attitudes. Attitudes have to do with the willingness of workers to perform tasks and activities. A motivated workforce does not necessarily

---

HOSPITALITY TIPS & CLIPS   *Ways to Say "Way to Go"*

Sometimes offering praise is harder than it should be. In a busy operation it's easy to forget to compliment and voice your appreciation. But praise can really make a team member's day. Here are some reminders of how to say, "Thanks, well done."

- I'm proud you're on my team.
- Congratulations on a terrific job.
- You're so helpful. Thank you!
- You keep improving. Well done.
- Thanks so much for your consistent effort.
- I really admire your perseverance.
- Your mood always lifts the team's spirits.
- Wow, what an incredible accomplishment!
- Good effort. You make us all look good.
- I have great confidence in you.

- You've grasped the concept well.
- Your customer service skills are sensational.
- Your sales results are outstanding.
- You're a valuable part of this team.
- Your efforts are really making a difference.
- You continue to delight our customers.
- You make the team's vision come alive.
- Your accomplishments inspire our team.
- Customers are noticing the efforts you're putting in.
- You're a champion!

Source: "Ways to Say 'Way to Go.'" *Hospitality News* (April 2001): p. 32. Courtesy of *Hospitality News.*

guarantee productivity. Productivity depends on psychological factors as well as engineering factors. Work area layout, division of tasks, tools to do the job, technology, and other factors are within the scope of workplace engineering. A combination of engineering design and management of behaviors is required to impact worker satisfaction and enhance productivity.

Job Design and Motivation

Job rotation—Moving an individual worker to different positions requiring varying tasks.

Job enlargement—Adding tasks to the existing job list for an individual worker.

Job rotation is a management technique of providing different forms of work with equal levels of responsibility. This technique is sometimes used to break the monotony of doing a single fragmented task. While this may offer variety, it is not necessarily a motivational technique for improved performance.

In these times of corporate downsizing, **job enlargement** is a popular alternative. Job enlargement involves adding more duties to an existing job. The additional duties do not usually include added responsibility and authority. Therefore, job enlargement is not a motivational technique. Sometimes managers inadvertently penalize good workers by adding additional responsibilities to their jobs. Managers do this because they know that the worker will be able to handle the additional assignments. However, the manager who does this actually discourages workers from becoming top performers.

Job enrichment—Adding authority and autonomy along with enhanced responsibility to the job list for an individual worker.

Job enrichment is a technique of restructuring a job to provide added autonomy, responsibility, and authority.[13] Job enrichment is more than just a job design approach toward motivation. It is also a means to improve productivity. This is an example of combining a workplace engineering approach with human motivation to achieve productivity enhancement. Job enrichment is a motivational job design method because it provides benefits to those workers who prove they are capable of more important positions based on their performance.

HOSPITALITY TIPS & CLIPS *Motivated Employees Are Essential for Customer Service*

Keeping your employees motivated to consistently provide high-quality customer service is a task just short of monumental for many companies. But it can be done, as long as you focus on one customer at a time. Here are a few tips:

Practice what you preach. If you want a motivated staff, you need to be motivated first. In all you do, are you continually assessing the customer service that you personally are giving to your customers? Unless you are "walking the walk," you won't be able to motivate your employees.

Hire the right people. The rule is either to hire smart or manage tough. Hiring smart also requires that you are motivated yourself. You can only attract people who are excited about what you do by being excited yourself. Make customer service and your expectations a part of the hiring interview. When training, make sure your employees understand your expectations for customer service.

Keep score. If you don't measure performance, your employees will be in a perpetual warm-up mode. Let employees know what they are being measured for and how it is relevant to them, customers, and your organization's bottom line.

Reward. Make sure you reward. When you overhear a server offer a sincere cheerful greeting to a customer, later say, "I really like what I'm hearing from you, and I can tell our customers like it too!" Don't neglect to offer a verbal thank-you to your dedicated employees. Then include a coupon as a tiny token of your appreciation in his next paycheck with a personal note. (A free car wash or video rental is enough.) At team meetings, share success stories with your other employees. "I can't wait to tell you what I've been observing!" People appreciate being acknowledged in front of their peers.

Source: "Motivated Employees are Essential for Customer Service." *Hospitality News* (August 2002): p. 17. Courtesy of *Hospitality News.*

PERSONALITY AND MOTIVATION

Personality traits— A person's preference for behavior given certain environmental stimuli. Considered to be both genetic and learned, it comprises a person's social comfort zone.

Perhaps the most influential individual motivator on a visceral level is what are referred to as **personality traits,** which means nothing more than a person's preference for behavior given certain environmental conditions. Because personality preferences are indicators of comfort levels for certain types of positions, human resource practitioners commonly use personality tests or temperament sorters as part of the pre-employment screening process. It should be noted, however, that practitioners should be familiar with the legal ramifications resulting from the use of such instruments before instituting policies to include such criteria, as will be discussed in Chapter 8.

Commonly used instruments to measure personality preferences include the Myers-Briggs and Kersey-Bates Temperament Sorters. The DISC instrument developed in 1958 is commonly used to measure preferences for managerial environments. While these psychological metrics do provide indicators of environmental preference, it is important to remember that they are not behavioral predictors. This is because people possess the ability to behave in a manner that is contrary to their personality preferences, even though such conditions may create levels of personal stress. This is why a careful review of case law relative to the specific service enterprise should be conducted by a legal professional prior to the implementation of such measurements in the process of making employment decisions. The legal aspects aside, however, these instruments appear to be both statistically valid and reliable.

The instruments measure preferences of persons with such traits as introversion and extroversion. For instance, an extroverted individual seems to have a preference for working with a variety of individuals as opposed to being restricted to an office environment. This factor is a big plus for hospitality front-line workers. However, most entertainers appear to be introverted, allowing an alter ego to emerge during a given performance. So, managers at a major theme park, for instance, would expect the introverts to render marvelous entertainment performances, but they would also realize that these individuals would be too emotionally drained to act in the capacity of "meeters and greeters" after the show. This task is best reserved for individuals with extroverted personality preferences.

Other personality factors include intuition, thinking, feeling, perceiving, judging, and sensing preferences for people who perform tasks. The managerial temperament instruments consider similar variables related to the practice of management in organizational environments. People often surprise those who administer personality instruments, as observed behaviors may mask personality preferences for a given individual.

SUMMARY

Managers prefer to work with motivated employees. When workers are motivated, managers may perform fewer tasks associated with "people management," which provides opportunities for the supervisor to focus more on leadership tasks. It is much easier and more fulfilling to lead people than it is to manage them. For this reason, managers and supervisors should make it their business to learn as much about applied behavior as possible in order to develop both the intuitive and analytical abilities to identify those factors that influence individuals and groups to be motivated to perform in constructive ways. Also, more than motivation is required to impact productivity. Workplace engineering issues must be combined with managing people to provide enhancements to productivity.

Some managers believe that demonstrating favoritism to certain workers will provide motivation for others to improve performance. The opposite is true. The individuals receiving preferential treatment will feel uncomfortable interacting with peers. The other workers will resent the preferential treatment and usually become less than constructive in their behaviors. Managers who are perceived by workers as playing favorites will eventually alienate all of the staff members in a work unit.

... *In the Real World* (Continued)

Well, as it turns out you did talk with Gloria, the director of housekeeping, and you did accept the job as evening shift manager. However, before you accepted the job, you made a deal with Gloria. You have permission from the hotel controller to pay the evening attendants shift pay instead of an hourly rate.

The attendants on your shift provide turndown service to the guest rooms in the hotel. The objective is for them to get as many rooms finished in the shortest period of time. By establishing a shift pay policy, you are now empowered to show your attendants the easiest way to complete their tasks in the shortest period of time. This is a win-win situation for the hotel, for you, and for them. They make the same money they would make in a 6-hour shift in as little as 4 hours, just by working smarter. You know this is a motivator as people who do this work usually have family obligations and are often working a second job. If you keep doing things like this, it won't be long before Gloria will be letting you move from her department for your next promotion.

QUESTIONS FOR DISCUSSION

1. Sometimes we use job design methods and other times we use individual and group methods of motivation. Sometimes we even combine the two. Which ones work the best?

2. Some people like the process theories of motivation more than the content theories. Do you think the process theories make more sense? Do you think they have anything in common with the content theories?

3. Some people say that money is definitely not a motivator. Is this true? Why or why not? Could we say that the meaning behind the money has anything to do with motivation?

MINI-CASE

You work as a server in an upscale dining room on the dinner shift. On one particular evening you were able to provide superlative service to your guests who were mostly great tippers. At the end of the evening you cashed out and learned that you made over $500 in gratuities. Instead of being greedy, you decided to tip the busser $100, and you gave the bartender and the captain $50 each. Then you walked back to the dish room and gave each dishwashing attendant $5 each for a total of $25. Your net gratuities for the evening were now down to $275.

Question:

How might you benefit from being so generous with your gratuities?

Hints:

1. The busser makes your job easier and provides you with table turnovers.

2. The captain influences the maître d' when it comes to seating and does wine and flambé service at your tables.

3. There never seems to be enough clean china, glass, and silver for you to provide service to your guests.

 KEY TERMS

Behavior modification theory	Hierarchy of needs theory	Management by objectives	Personality traits
Equity theory	Job enlargement	Motivation	Positive reinforcement
Expectancy theory	Job enrichment	Negative reinforcement	Two-factor theory
	Job rotation		

CHAPTER QUIZ

1. Motivation is the willingness to do something. **T F**
2. Leadership and motivation go hand in hand. **T F**
3. Motivational factors are the same for all people. **T F**
4. Some people are motivated by money and what it means to them. **T F**
5. Negative reinforcement is a form of punishment. **T F**
6. Low-wage earners are more focused on security needs. **T F**
7. The two-factor theory says all needs are motivators. **T F**
8. Perceptions of fairness impact the motivations of people. **T F**
9. Job enrichment includes more authority and responsibility. **T F**

ENDNOTES

1. D. V. Tesone, *Tactical Strategies for Service Industry Management: How to Do It* (2003), Boston: Pearson.
2. Ibid.
3. Bradley G. Jackson, "Art for Management's Sake?" *Management Communication Quarterly* 14, no. 3 (February 2001): 484.
4. Charles R. McConnell, "The Manager and Continuing Education," *The Health Care Manager* 21, no. 2 (December 2002): 72.
5. Ibid.
6. Barry Eustace, "Universal Manager," *Hospitality* (October 2002): 34.
7. Ibid.
8. Ibid.
9. Diane S. Grimes, "Challenging the Status Quo?" *Management Communication Quarterly* 15, no. 3 (February 2002): 381.
10. Lyle Sussman, "Organizational Politics: Tactics, Channels, and Hierarchical Roles," *Journal of Business Ethics* 40, no. 4 (November 2002): 313.
11. Gita De Souza, "A Study of the Influence of Promotions on Promotion Satisfaction and Expectations of Future Promotions among Managers," *Human Resource Development Quarterly* 13, no. 3 (Fall 2002): 325.

12. David A. Whetten, "A Social Actor Conception of Organizational Identity and Its Implications for the Study of Organizational Reputation," *Business and Society* 41, no. 4 (December 2002): 393.

13. Pursey P. Heugens, "The Confines of Stakeholder Management: Evidence from the Dutch Manufacturing Sector," *Journal of Business Ethics* 40, no. 4 (November 2002): 387.

CHAPTER FIVE
Supervisory Communication

OBJECTIVES

By the end of this chapter, readers will be able to:

1. Understand and use the communication model.
2. Understand the importance of effective listening.
3. Recognize effective feedback techniques.
4. Identify formal and informal communication networks.
5. Understand the importance of multidirectional communication flows.

In the Real World...

You are an audiovisual (A/V) technician for a convention center. You have been working in the department for about one year. In the past the A/V manager, Matt, has worked around your school schedule. However, 2 weeks ago, your schedule changed to include conflicts with your classes. You stopped by Matt's office to discuss this, and he kind of blew you off by saying, "Oh yeah, it was just a mistake on the part of the assistant. Work with me and I'll fix it next week." So, you worked with him. The next week, the schedule had the same conflicts. You entered Matt's office and he was apparently very stressed. He barked, "I can't do everything for everyone around here! You have to work with me on this." You felt a little disgruntled at this treatment, but you complied with the schedule. Upon arriving to work today, you notice that your scheduled hours have not changed from last week. Feeling a little uncertain on approaching Matt for a third time, you decide to visit the employee relations manager in the human resources office.

Nadia was just promoted to employee relations manager from an operations management position. You worked with her when she was a convention services manager and feel comfortable talking with her about your scheduling situation. She listens closely to what you have to say about the past couple of weeks. She leans toward you as you speak and takes notes. She acknowledges your sentences and paraphrases your descriptions to ensure her understanding of the issues. Her facial expressions demonstrate genuine concern for your situation between work and school. She behaves in an objective, yet caring manner, and at the end of your explanation, paraphrases everything that has happened with the schedule and your meetings with Matt over the past 2 weeks. She ends the meeting by saying, "Give me some time to discuss this with Matt, and I will let you know what to expect. I will have an answer for you by the time you start work tomorrow, so be sure to visit with me just before starting your shift. Or if you like I can call you at home." You agree to stop by tomorrow and thank her for her time.

After your departure from Nadia's office at about 6:00 p.m., she is ready to leave for the day. She stops by the human resources director's office to chat on her way out. She says, "You know, I just don't understand it; when I worked in operations I ran around all day long to keep up with everything. Now that I have this job, it seems so much easier, since I just sit here and handle people's problems. But when I go home at the end of the day, like I am totally wiped out. Much more so than when I used to run around putting out fires all day long." The HR director gives Nadia a knowing smile and a nod of the head. She says, "You are experiencing emotional energy drain." "What's that all about?" says Nadia. "Look," the HR director answers, "you sit here all day long actively listening to negative situations. While you think you are doing nothing, by the end of the day you are emotionally and mentally drained from this activity. It's hard work to listen to people's problems." "Oh, I get it," says Nadia, "Brain Drain!" (To be continued)

Communication—
The process of exchanging ideas for the purpose of sharing information and concepts.

The most important tool for a manager or supervisor is the ability to effectively engage in communication activities with other individuals. A person may know all there is to know about supervision and still not be an effective supervisor if he does not possess a solid base of communication skills.

There are many definitions of communication in organizations. This chapter presents a simplified definition for the reader. **Communication** may be defined as the sharing and understanding of information among individuals.[1] While this sounds simple, the process of engaging in effective communication is really quite complex. This is due to the individuality of people. Individuality impacts personal perception. Each person perceives information in different ways. Therefore, while everyone in a group of people may hear the same message, that message will mean different things to different people. A perfect example of this is the old game of passing a message along a line of people. Each person whispers a message in the ear of the next person in line. At the end, the message repeated by the last person in line is usually very different than the original message. Take this phenomenon and multiply it times the numerous incidents of communication that take place among people in an organization. It becomes evident that organizational communication is a very complicated topic. Consultants tell us that lack of effective communication is the most prominent problem in organizations.[2]

THE COMMUNICATION PROCESS

A model for organizational communication is presented in Figure 5.1. Notice that the model starts with the **sender.** The Sender thinks of an idea. This idea is merely a thought in the Sender's mind. The Sender must **encode** the thought into a message. This means the Sender is using words to symbolize the concepts within the thought. After the Sender identifies the words or symbols to be used to represent the thought, the Sender chooses a **Medium** for the message. A Medium may be written formats such as memos or letters. A Medium could also be electronic, such as a telephone, intercom, or email. A Medium could be verbal, such as an interview, a meeting, or an informal discussion. All of these examples represent means through which a Sender packages and sends a message. Since the message is packaged for the Receiver of the message, the package is known as the Medium. The Medium is the format used for broadcasting a message to intended Receivers. The Medium carries the message to the **Receiver,** who then must **decode** the message. The process of encoding into a Medium and decoding by the Receiver comprises

Sender—The person with an idea who wants to send a message to someone else.

Encode—To convert an idea into symbols for communication to a receiver in the communication process.

Medium—The mechanism used to carry a message through a channel in the communication process.

Receiver—The intended recipient of a message in the communication process.

Decode—To mentally comprehend a message sent by a sender in the communication process.

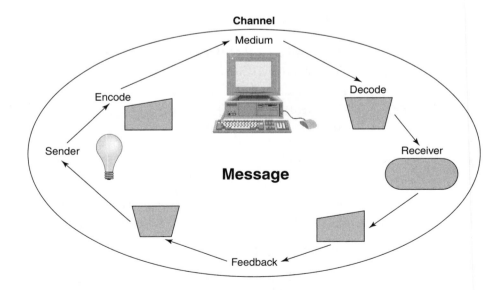

Figure 5–1.

Channel—The directional flow of communications.

Feedback—The process of reinforcing awareness of an interactive activity.

the **channel** of the message. After the Receiver decodes the message, a **feedback** loop is used for the Receiver to respond to the message. The feedback loop closes the cycle. This permits the process of Sender, Medium, and Receiver to begin again.

Consider an example to demonstrate the Communication Model. A manager has decided to enact a change in staff scheduling practices. The manager notices that individuals prefer specific days off for various reasons. In the interest of fairness, she develops an idea that will allow members of the staff to request days off before the schedule is made for the following week. So far, this is just a concept in the mind of the manager. Now she must put the idea into words (encoding). She jots down a few notes concerning the idea. Next the manager must decide on how the message will be sent to the staff. She decides to announce the new practice in an upcoming shift meeting and to follow up with a printed notice concerning staff requests. In this case, there are two Mediums; one is the meeting (verbal), and the other is a notice (written). A shift meeting is scheduled for Wednesday. At the meeting, the manager presents the new procedure for requesting days off prior to each week's posting of the schedule. She looks at the facial expressions and body language of the participants to ensure that all understand the new procedure (feedback). Finally, the manager asks if anyone has any questions about the procedure (feedback). A member of the staff indicates that he has a question. At this point, the feedback loop is closed and a new communication process is about to begin. The person with the question becomes the Sender. He thinks about what he wants to ask, finds words to encode his message, verbalizes the words in the form of a question (Medium), and watches the manager (Receiver) for a response (feedback). As the manager decodes the question, she prepares a response; thus, the manager is starting a new communication process as the Sender.

This is the Communication Model at work. We communicate so quickly that we don't recognize the steps involved in our communications. We develop ideas, encode them, place them in a medium, send them for decoding, watch or listen for feedback, and await a response in fractions of seconds.

WHY ARE COMMUNICATION SKILLS IMPORTANT FOR MANAGERS?

If the practice of management involves accomplishing the objectives of the organization through the activities of others, then the ability to effectively communicate is crucial for the success of the manager. Imagine knowing all there is to know about the field of management. Also, imagine how ineffective you would be with that knowledge if you could not talk, write, or otherwise communicate with the workers. No matter how much knowledge a person has in the field of management, if that person is unable to communicate with other people, the tasks and goals will not be accomplished. Therefore, that person will not be a successful manager.

LISTENING SKILLS

How well do most people listen? According to some experts, the majority of individuals listen at an effectiveness rate of 25 percent.[3] Also, the experts indicate that individuals who work in senior management positions spend as

much as 85 percent of their communication time listening to other people.[4] It is a fact that listening skills top the list of effective managerial communication skills. While effective listening is the most important communication skill, it is, perhaps, the least taught skill.

One reason for possessing effective listening skills is that you, as the manager, will make decisions based on information presented to you. You will be involved in the following types of listening scenarios:

- Problem solving
- Conflict resolution
- Performance evaluations
- Resource allocation
- Brainstorming
- Strategic planning
- Organizing departments
- Customer satisfaction indicators
- Scheduling
- Assigning duties
- Hiring personnel
- Coaching and discipline
- Policies and rules
- Practices and procedures
- Other activities to support your staff members

Each of these activities requires effective listening skills for maximum decision making. Therefore, the smart manager is in the listening business. As

HOSPITALITY TIPS & CLIPS *Tips for Becoming an Effective Communicator*

One of the most valuable skills a manager can acquire is to become an effective communicator. Ineffective communication often results in poor cooperation and coordination; lower productivity; undercurrents of tension, gossip, and rumors; and increased turnover and absenteeism.

Experience shows there are many ways managers can improve internal communications. Here are eight things to try:

1. Understand that communication is a two-way street. It involves giving information and getting feedback from employees. It isn't finished when information is given.
2. Put more emphasis on face-to-face communication with employees. Don't rely mainly on bulletin boards, memos, and other written communication.
3. Each time you give an instruction, ask yourself if the message is clear. Most vagueness is caused by failing to be specific. Don't just tell an employee to "show more interest" in her work. If an employee spends too much time chatting with others, be more specific about it.

4. View information as "service to" employees and not "power over" them.
5. Take time to listen to your employees; show respect for them when they speak. They'll feel like part of the team and will tend to be more dedicated and productive. Ask questions to show interest and clarify points.
6. Don't just talk open-door policy. Show it by walking around and talking to your employees. Allow people to disagree and to come up with new ideas.
7. Conduct one-on-one meetings. Ask each employee to tell you how you can help him do a better job, then how the employee can help you do a better job.
8. Concentrate on building credibility with employees. Managers who lack credibility and fail to create a climate of trust and openness aren't believed, no matter how hard they try to communicate.

Source: "A Little Help for Managers." *Hospitality News* (February 2002): p. 23. Courtesy of *Hospitality News.*

managers assume higher levels of responsibility, their listening skills become more important.

BARRIERS TO EFFECTIVE LISTENING

Effective listening requires time, energy, concentration, technique, and objectivity. Listening actively actually requires more effort than talking or writing. Many managers think they are actively listening to people, when they are, in fact, creating barriers to effective listening. Some barriers to effective listening are listed below:

- Diverted attention
- Mood and experience

- Judgmental attitude
- Noise (distractions)
- Planning the response
- Lack of interest
- Failure to ask probing questions

Following are examples of a few typical scenarios.

An individual arranges to meet with the manager. As the individual approaches the manager's office at the appointed time, the manager is on the phone. The manager waves the person into the office without missing any of the phone conversation. The person sits down and waits for the phone conversation to end. Finally, the manager hangs up the phone and addresses the person sitting in the office. As the person begins to speak, the manager shuffles through papers on the desk. This is an example of diverted attention. The manager is not fully listening to that person, who is likely to feel uncomfortable with the lack of attention.

A person enters the manager's office only to find that the manager is under severe stress. The manager is obviously fatigued and distracted. This is an example of mood as a barrier to effective listening. Perhaps the person wants to talk to the manager about a problem that has been recently addressed by many other workers. Upon hearing the topic of discussion, the manager indicates disinterest in what the person has to say; the manager has already "heard it all." This is an example of experience as a barrier to effective listening.

A person is attempting to explain to the manager the reason that some action was taken. The manager appears to be closed minded. This is an example of judgmental attitude as a barrier to effective listening.

There is a small meeting with four participants. One participant stands up and gazes out the window. Another person is doodling. Another is tapping a pencil. These are examples of noise as a barrier to effective listening. In this case "noise" does not necessarily have to mean noise in the audible sense. Any distraction, even silent distractions, creates a form of distraction called noise.

Mood and Experience

Most individuals have high and low spans of attention throughout the workday. Some individuals are "morning people," others are "late bloomers." Peak times are those during which the individual is energized and focused. Since effective listening requires focused energy, it may be appropriate for managers and supervisors to schedule discussions during peak periods. Often workers will approach the manager during an inconvenient time. The manager now has a dilemma. If he takes the time to talk with the worker, it is possible that he may be distracted and not listen effectively. On the other hand, if he does not talk with the worker, the worker may feel that the manager does not value the worker's existence. Perhaps an appropriate response on the part of the manager would be to reinforce that the worker's feedback is important; however, due to the current level of activities, it is an inappropriate time for the discussion. The manager might further state that the discussion should take place when both parties are able to effectively concentrate on the topic.

The manager would then proceed to schedule an appointment for the discussion.

Planning the Response

One expert describes the two-person conversation as a multiple-party monologue. In this scenario, both parties are concentrating on what it is they want to say. Both start talking, and the first person to draw a breath is declared the listener.[5] However, this person is not really listening. Instead, she is mentally rehearsing a response to interject when the speaker stops talking.

This is often the case in organizational discussions. Planning the response is a common barrier to effective listening. When this occurs, the speaker should reiterate the message until the listener indicates that it has been heard by responding appropriately. Another technique for overcoming this barrier is to permit the intended listener to talk first. After all has been said, the barrier of mental rehearsal should be overcome.

Lack of Attention

In every department there seems to be one or two workers who spend large amounts of time discussing seemingly unimportant issues with the manager. The manager eventually becomes programmed to believe that these people will waste the manager's time. In these cases, the manager must work to overcome this judgmental barrier. To do this she must assume the optimistic view that, one of these times, this person is going to focus on an issue of substance. The manager thus expends effort to listen effectively, just in case this becomes that opportunity. A word of caution to the inexperienced manager: Some individuals prefer talking to working. The manager must determine if the worker's visit is a work avoidance tactic. If it is suspected that this is true, the manager should suggest that the worker schedule another time for the discussion.

OTHER FACTORS INFLUENCING COMMUNICATION

Formal and Informal Communication

Formal communications take place when people are representing the interests of the organization as part of their appointed duties. A manager who conducts a performance appraisal is communicating formally because the manager is acting in an appointed capacity and is engaging in a form of communication that will be documented for the record. Other types of formal communications include memos, letters, meetings, bulletin board postings, announcements, policies, procedures, standards, and newsletters.

Informal communications exist outside the mainstream of the organization's communication channels. A commonly cited example of informal communications is known as the "**grapevine**."[6] Practically all members of an organization (minus a few senior managers) participate in the grapevine. It is the informal communication process that takes place among people within the organization or industry. Usually, the grapevine consists of rumors, innuendo, speculation, and hearsay information. Topics of communication may

Grapevine—A form of informal communication that includes activities such as gossip or rumors.

extend beyond organizational issues into people's personal lives. The grapevine is often labeled as the "rumor mill" or the "word on the street." At times, the grapevine may be a source of accurate information that travels faster than the flow of information in the formal communication process. Regardless of the accuracy of information traveling through the grapevine, managers are advised to pay close attention to what is being communicated. The grapevine is an important source of information concerning the attitudes and morale of workers in the organization. Some studies indicate that the speed and accuracy of information within the grapevine increases significantly in organizations with poor formal communication flow.[7] The opposite seems to be true for organizations with open, honest, and free-flowing channels of communication.

Managers also possess opportunities to engage in constructive informal communications with workers. As a matter of fact, experienced managers often report that they get much more done while acting informally than they do through formal communication modes.

Nonverbal Communication

A good deal of information gained during face-to-face interactions comes from nonverbal cues. These include body language, facial expressions, eye contact, posture, and gestures. Some research indicates that as much as 75 percent of information is gained through observing nonverbal cues.[8] Interpreting nonverbal behavior is often subjective. Cultural differences provide varied interpretations associated with nonverbal cues. For instance, for people of western European cultures, lack of eye contact may indicate dishonesty. For individuals from other cultures, the same action may symbolize respect for authority.[9]

CHOOSING MESSAGE MEDIA

Recall from the Communication Model that the Sender encodes a message into a medium for transmission to the Receiver. Media may take the form of informal conversations, email, meetings, notes, memos, letters, and other forms of transmission. Most forms of media may be classified in one of two major categories. The first category is written media. This would include electronic media such as email. The second category is verbal interaction.

Like most people, managers have a tendency to avoid confrontation. For this reason, some managers prefer placing messages in written format as opposed to engaging in verbal interaction. In many instances, putting messages into writing may be less constructive than face-to-face interaction. There are many reasons to avoid written forms of communication. Face-to-face interaction provides both parties with opportunities to extract information through nonverbal cues as discussed in a previous chapter. Personal interaction often adds to the perception of importance of the topic of communication. Also, people feel important when they are invited to interact with a manager or supervisor. Finally, a familiarity often develops as a result of personal interaction. As long as professional distinctions are maintained, familiarity makes the work environment comfortable. Therefore, it is suggested that managers take every appropriate opportunity to communicate verbally with members of the staff.

There are occasions that call for written communication media. Written messages have posterity; that is, they last for long periods of time and provide future reference materials. Also, written communications provide documentation of an event for future reference or as a matter of record. More formal occasions call for written media. For example, a worker who has demonstrated superior performance may appreciate a formal letter of congratulations from the manager. One recommended technique is to send hand-written thank-you notes to staff members for appropriate reasons. Finally, conversations or meetings may be clarified through written follow-up documents.

Managers must decide on the appropriate communication media for each set of circumstances. Whenever possible, it is suggested that personal interaction be chosen as the medium for communication. Some circumstances may warrant verbal interaction with written follow-up correspondence. The problem with overreliance on written communications is the perceived lack of importance of memos and other correspondence in most organizations. This is due to the paper avalanche and information overload associated with written messages in organizations.

DIRECTIONAL FLOWS OF ORGANIZATIONAL COMMUNICATIONS

Recall the communication channels cited in the Communication Model. The medium is the means of message transmission. The channel is the direction of transmission throughout the organization's hierarchy (organization chart). Many managers are familiar with the traditional downward direction of communication. The managers send directives downward through the organizational chart, and workers adhere to the directions. Managers should be aware

---

HOSPITALITY TIPS & CLIPS   *Are You an Effective Manager?*

Sure, you know how well your employees perform on their jobs. But how effective are you for your employees? One way to find out is to gauge your staff's perceptions of you. Human resources experts suggest that you (or an objective third party) ask these types of questions of your staff:

- How well do I give employees feedback?
- How well do I keep them informed of what's going on in the organization?
- How well do I support their ideas and suggestions?
- Do employees feel I have enough job knowledge?

- Am I friendly and helpful?
- Do I give employees the equipment and training that they need to be successful?
- Do I treat all employees fairly and not give special preferences to some?
- Do I listen to my employees' suggestions?
- Do I know my employees—what their interests, goals, strengths are? What they like to do and what they don't enjoy doing?

Source: "Are You an Effective Manager?" *Hospitality News* (April 2002): p. 29. Courtesy of *Hospitality News.*

---

that effective communication requires flows of information in multiple directions. Figure 5.2 illustrates the directional flow of communications.

Notice that communications flow in many directions in a healthy organization. Directions include upward, downward, lateral, and diagonal flows. Upward flows should include open feedback to managers who support those working on the line. Lateral flows provide organization of tasks among operating departments. Downward diagonal flows provide support information from higher levels in the organization to line workers. Upward diagonal flows provide feedback to diagonal support networks.

SUMMARY

Communication skills are vital to a manager's ability to accomplish the objectives of the organization through the actions of others. Therefore, the responsibility for communicating effectively in all directions lies squarely with the

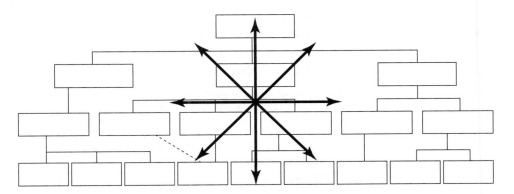

Figure 5–2.

immediate supervisor. Messages must be honest and appeal to the perceptions of others to be effective. While written communications are sometimes appropriate, they are often less effective than verbal interactions. The Communication Model demonstrates the development of the message by the Sender, the transmission of the message through a medium, the sending of the message through the channel, the decoding of the message by the Receiver, and the feedback loop. The feedback loop closes one communication sequence and starts another sequence. Therefore, the feedback loop goes beyond clarifying the Receiver's interpretation of the message. The grapevine is an example of an informal communication system. In a healthy organization, it is recognized that complaints and grievances are useful and important parts of the communication process.

... In the Real World (Continued)

On her way in to work the next morning, Nadia stops by Matt's office to discuss your scheduling situation.

"Hey, Nadia," says Matt, "how's the new job going in HR?" Nadia replies, "Good, Matt. As a matter of fact, that is why I'm here. I want to talk with you about the schedule for one of your staff members." "Oh, that," says Matt, "I just needed to move a few people around for 3 weeks to handle some business and a sick leave." Nadia says, "So, why didn't you just tell your staff member that?" "I did!" exclaims Matt. "That's not how I heard it," says Nadia. " I heard that in the first week it was a mistake by your assistant. In the second week you complained about having to accommodate everyone—" Matt interrupts with, "Well, you know how hectic it gets down here. By the time the second shift starts, we're in the weeds. I don't have time to explain everything." Nadia responds by saying, "You don't have time **not** to explain things. How much time will it take you to replace this staff member?"

"You have a great employee here," continues Nadia, "one of your best staff members, as far as I can tell. Put yourself in that person's position. Don't you think this individual has a right to an explanation, especially with a track record of cooperation over the past year?" "Yeah, I guess you're right," admits Matt, "it's just a matter of effectively communicating with the staff." Nadia says, "Matt, you're a good manager. You are a young go-getter. But you can't manage people the way the old-timers managed you. You have to show them that you care by taking a little time, no matter when, to listen and explain things to them. This is especially true for your good ones." "Thanks, Nadia (. . . I think)," says Matt. "It's real easy to forget how it felt when we were working in the trenches for the Neanderthals."

"So can I tell this staff member to visit you for a focused discussion at the start of the second shift today?" asks Nadia. "Sure," says Matt, "I'll make things right."

QUESTIONS FOR DISCUSSION

1. Have you ever taken a course in active listening? If you were to teach such a course, what would you tell the supervisors?

2. Consider the scenarios presented in this chapter. Have you ever experienced one of them? How did that make you feel? How would you have behaved if you were the one in charge?

3. Nadia chose to pay a personal visit to Matt in the "Real World" vignette. Why did she do that and why did she choose to visit at a certain time of

day? Would you have made the same decision, even if it meant a personal confrontation with Matt about his supervisory style?

MINI-CASE

Lilly had just taken over as the food and beverage director of a small hotel with one restaurant, room service, and a small lobby lounge. There are three managers, one for each outlet. There is also one assistant manager for each outlet.

As she looked around the office, Lilly was not able to locate a copy of the strategic plan for F&B operations. She couldn't find any training programs or steps of service standards. There were no logbooks, no meeting minutes, and no signs of shift meetings. Employees just seemed to show up for work and do whatever they thought was the right thing to do. There was no record of guest comments or guest service indices, but the general manager told her that business in the outlets had declined significantly. As she observed the operation, she noticed numerous communication breakdowns among the lounge, room service, and restaurant managers. It seemed there was a shortage of wait staff in the outlets. The existing servers were not familiar with steps of service and menu items. Morale among the staff seemed low. They seemed to resent the managers.

Question:

Why do you think there was a shortage of wait staff, low morale, and resentment of the managers?

Hint:

What evidence do you see of poor managerial communications?

 KEY TERMS

Channel	Encode	Grapevine	Receiver
Communication	Feedback	Medium	Sender
Decode			

CHAPTER QUIZ

1. Effective communications are complex.   T   F
2. It is impossible for a person to supervise without communication skills.   T   F
3. Formal communications follow directional flows in the organization.   T   F
4. Individuals all have the same perceptions.   T   F
5. There are many barriers to effective communications.   T   F
6. Communication begins with an idea in the sender's mind.   T   F
7. A medium carries a message through a channel.   T   F

8. A receiver has no interaction with the sender of a message.   **T**   **F**

9. The grapevine is an example of informal communication.   **T**   **F**

10. Effective listening is the most important skill for supervisors.   **T**   **F**

ENDNOTES

1. Robert H. Stowers, "Top Ten Tips in Teaching Communication to Executive MBA Students," *Business Communication Quarterly* 65, no. 3 (September 2002): 65.

2. Ibid.

3. Ralph Nichols and L. A. Stevens, *Are you listening?* (New York: McGraw-Hill, 1957).

4. Ibid.

5. Jane Whitney Gibson and Richard M. Hodgetts, *Organizational Communications: A Managerial Perspective* (New York: Holt Rinehart & Winston, 1986).

6. Ibid.

7. Jane Whitney Gibson, *Supervisory Challenge: Principles and Practices* (Upper Saddle River, NJ: Merrill/Prentice Hall, 1990).

8. Ibid.

9. Dana V. Tesone, "Development of a Human Resources Module for Sustainable Tourism: A Template for Future Modules," *International Journal of Hospitality Management* 25, no. 2 (2004).

CHAPTER SIX
Employee Training

OBJECTIVES

At the end of this chapter, readers will be able to:

1. Understand the needs analysis process preceding training activities.
2. Identify useful techniques for skills and knowledge training.
3. Recognize commonly used training terminology.
4. Understand the role of the supervisor in the training process.

In the Real World . . .

You have just been hired as a reservations agent at the central reservations center for a cruise line. On your first day of work, the human resources office processed all of your paperwork and provided you with a 2-hour orientation program. The program consisted of a few out-dated video presentations and some general information about the company history, policies, and procedures, as well as benefits package options. You were then sent to the reservations center to begin work.

Now, as you walk around the halls, you finally find the reservations center after asking for directions from one of the employees in the hallway. As you enter the center, you notice that the room is buzzing with about 25 agents seated at open-space desks, wearing headphones and talking with travel agents and prospective passengers by phone. Standing behind every five or so agents is a headset-adorned supervisor who listens in on random conversations. Everyone is working at a frenetic pace, unaware of your presence as you stand near the door-way for what seems like an eternity. You walk further into the room to ask the nearest supervisor for the manager. Without interrupting her task or acknowledging you, she points over her shoulder to a glass-enclosed office at the rear of the work area. As you approach the office, you enter through the open door to find a middle-aged woman talking on the phone, who is obviously engaged in a heated discussion with someone else in the organization. Without los-ing the stride of her conversation, she points at a chair in front of her desk for you to take a seat. As you wait for her phone argument to come to an end, you take note of the disheveled office space with mounds of computer printouts strewn about.

Finally, the woman ends her phone conversation with a threatening comment before slam-ming the phone receiver down. She looks at you inquisitively, so you say, "Hi Fran, remember me? I interviewed with you a few weeks ago." "Oh yeah," she says, "HR finally got you processed, huh? It's about time, it's a madhouse in here!" She presses the intercom button and says, "Frank, come to the office, please." Frank, one of the supervisors, arrives and is intro-duced to you. You follow him to the work area. He says, "Sit here and watch Mary, she is one of my best agents." Mary says hello and you pull out a notepad. She says, "What are you doing?" You say, "I thought I would take notes." She replies, "Whatever, I wish I had thought of that when I started."

After a few days of this type of "training," you are placed at your own terminal to begin tak-ing reservations. (To be continued)

Training—Imparting knowledge and skills required for perfor-mance.

Providing appropriate levels of knowledge and skills is the essence of **training** in the workplace. The primary responsibility for training belongs to the im-mediate supervisor. In organizations where training managers are employed, the supervisor remains the person with ultimate responsibility for training workers. The objective of training is to provide a transfer of knowledge and skills to the worker. This means that the learning received during training is applied directly on the job. Effective training methods will have an impact on individuals' knowledge, skills, and behaviors.

Modifying knowledge, skills, and behaviors is relatively easy when com-pared to the task of changing people's attitudes. It is not the purpose of train-ing to change attitudes. Therefore, training should not be considered as a solution to solving attitude problems. In fact, the only time training is consid-ered as a solution is when a training problem exists, such as hiring new em-ployees without appropriate levels of technical skills. A training problem is defined as a negative gap between actual performance and standards for performance due to the knowledge and skills of a worker. This called a "learning gap." A learning gap is identified through a process known as needs analysis or needs assessment.

NEEDS ANALYSIS

The purpose of needs analysis is to determine whether or not a training problem exists in an organization. Examining the symptoms of performance problems does this. The hardest part of the problem-solving process is to identify the root problem from a list of symptoms. Many top managers make the mistake of throwing training programs at problems that are either organizational or workplace engineering problems. The training program will inevitably fail to solve these types of problems, and the senior manager will often abandon all training and fire the training manager. When an appropriate needs analysis is performed, the analyst is looking for a gap between knowledge and skills on one hand and standards for performance on the other. This is called a competency gap or learning gap. If a competency gap is identified, a training problem exists. Once the training problem is verified, trainers proceed to design, develop, implement, evaluate, and reinforce the training program.

COMPETENCE

Competence—The ability to function effectively and efficiently in a position.

There are four stages of **competence** to be identified when assessing the knowledge and skills of workers to be trained. The four stages are as follows:

- **Unconscious incompetence**—The stage in which the worker does not possess required knowledge and skills and does not know what knowledge and skills are required.
- **Conscious incompetence**—The stage in which the worker knows what learning is needed to perform the job and realizes the lack of knowledge and skills.
- **Conscious competence**—The stage in which the skills are new to the worker and the worker performs the skills slowly and deliberately.
- **Unconscious competence**—The stage in which the worker knows the skills well and can perform them quickly without deliberate concentration.

TYPES OF TRAINING

Various training methods are used to deliver learning. The type of training required and the nature of the learning outcomes for the training program determine these methods. Categories of training content are as follows:

- **Orientation**—Provides information to new employees for the purpose of assimilating them into the culture of the organization. Classroom settings and tours are commonly used for this purpose.

HOSPITALITY TIPS & CLIPS *The Benefits of a Structured Job Training Program*
By Adam Eisen

Instituting a structured training program will help you run your business efficiently and ultimately keep more money in your pocket. Studies show that employees not only need structure in the workplace environment, but actually desire it. These same studies also indicate that employees who have more structure at their job tend to be happier and remain longer with their company.

Therefore, it is vital to institute a well-structured training program as a solid foundation for employee-dependent businesses like those in the foodservice industry.

Carefully plan your training program. Throwing a new employee "into the fire" and expecting him/her to "learn by doing" creates numerous inefficiencies, which ultimately hurts your business. Prepare training programs so employees know exactly what is expected of them every day. The program should be specific and include the time each task is to be started and approximately how long it should take. Training programs should clearly outline goals and expectations both for the teacher (experienced employee) and the student (new employee).

As part of your training program, employees hired to perform one specific job should also cross-train for other jobs so they can assist in other areas where workflow is experiencing a crunch. This makes you less vulnerable to staffing shortages and dependence on one employee, which ultimately keeps the power of control in the hands of you, the employer.

In addition, include as part of your training program (and regular job criteria) the mandatory use of daily and weekly task checklists, which are vital for maintaining your company's high standards. Not only do checklists help maintain the standards of current employees, but also they help during turnover when a new employee replaces an existing employee. Without specific task checklists, job standards often slide, are improperly judged as unimportant and eliminated, or are just plain "forgotten" during employee turnover.

Finally, as part of a structured training program, a job description outlining the specific requirements and expectations must be designed for each position. The new employee must read and sign a job description acknowledging comprehension, which will prevent any further misunderstandings about the job duties.

Instituting a properly structured training program is the key for developing an efficient labor force. As a direct result, you will build a strong and knowledgeable team that will remain loyal for years on end. If you are spending too much time and money on labor, or feel your workforce is not running on all cylinders, my advice is to start at the beginning to rectify the end result.

Source: Adam Eisen. "The benefits of a structured job training program." *Hospitality News* (December 2002–January 2003): p. 13. Courtesy of *Hospitality News.*

- **Product knowledge**—Provides an overview of products and services provided by the organization. Classroom settings and tours are commonly used techniques.
- **Mechanical/technical skills**—Involves the use of hand-eye coordination to perform technical tasks. On-the-job training (OJT) methods combined with classroom and vestibule training are commonly used.

- **Administrative/technical skills**—Involves forms, paperwork, and computerized procedures for processing tasks within departments of the organization. Classroom settings are commonly used for this type of training.

- **Management/professional skills**—Includes abstract concepts associated with analysis and professional practices. Classroom settings are commonly used.

Following are various training delivery techniques:

- **Classroom setting**—The use of a meeting room away from the work area for knowledge and skills training

- **On-the-job training**—Training that occurs in the work area during "live" operations

- **Vestibule training**—A type of simulation training that occurs away from the work area for the practice of new skills

- **Tours**—Visits to areas of the organization to gain familiarity with operations in other departments as part of product knowledge training

- **Combinations**—Use of two or more of the training techniques listed

DEVELOPMENT AND EVALUATION OF TRAINING

The learning objectives drive the development and implementation of the training program. The objectives state the intended outcomes of the training. The objectives should be specific, measurable, challenging, and attainable. It is equally important that the trainer and the learners clearly understand the objectives for every training program. It is also imperative for the trainer to convince the learners of the personal benefits that will be experienced as a result of the training program. This is called WIFM (What's in it for me?). This is a crucial aspect to delivering training to adult learners.

Evaluation of Training Programs

All things are measurable, and training outcomes are no exception. The criteria for measuring training include cost/benefit to the organization, accomplishment of objectives, and personal improvement in the behavior and morale of workers. All of these things can be measured in quantifiable and qualitative terms.

Repetition

Repetition is the mother of learning. A trainer cannot be too repetitive. The golden rule of training is shown in Figure 6.1.

Feedback

Feedback is the breakfast of champions. Plenty of positive feedback should be provided throughout the training program. When in training mode, the supervisor is acting as a coach to the trainees.

STEPS TO PROVIDING EFFECTIVE TRAINING PROGRAMS

Knowledge—The information possessed by an individual.

Skills—Those demonstrated abilities of workers to contribute to the production of products and services in an organization.

All training may be placed into three categories: **knowledge** training, **skills** training, and a combination of knowledge and skills training.

There are four steps in delivering knowledge training. They are as follows:

1. Introduction/overview—Preview activities, WIFM, learning objectives, announce test.
2. Content—Three to five main points, subpoints for each main point, questions and conversation, encourage participation.
3. Test knowledge—Test for success. Provide positive feedback. If the test is an oral test, choose people who are likely to answer successfully.
4. Summary/conclusion—Review discussions, congratulate participants, provide preview of next session.

Knowledge training is usually conducted in a classroom setting. Trainers should realize that many individuals have had a negative training or educational experience. For this reason, it is important for trainers to overcome

```
TELL THEM WHAT YOU ARE GOING TO TELL THEM.
TELL THEM WHAT YOU ARE TELLING THEM.
THEN . . .
TELL THEM WHAT YOU TOLD THEM.
```

Figure 6–1. The golden rule of training.

original resistance on the part of learners. The underlying objective of the trainer is to make every training session an enjoyable experience for the learners.

An understanding of adult learning theory developed by researcher Malcolm Knowles and others will enhance the ability of the trainer to provide programs and formats that appeal to learners.[1] The researchers contend that adults learn what they need to know and prefer experiential training techniques. One factor for consideration in training implementation is the element of participation. Trainers should try to get some form of participation early in the session. One rule states that the trainer should seek some form of audience response within the first 5 minutes of a presentation, even if the response is as simple as asking people to raise their hands. Trainers are cautioned to avoid training design that forces the audience into passive roles.

There are three keys to providing effective skills training. They are: tell, show, and do. Tell the learners how to perform the task. Show the learners how to perform the task. Let the learners do the task for practice. The five steps for effective skills training are as follows:

1. Introduction/overview—Preview activities, WIFM, learning objectives, announce test.

2. Content—Three to five main points, subpoints for each main point, questions and conversation, encourage participation.

3. Demonstration—Show the learners how to perform the skill, demonstrate a small segment of the skill application, work slowly and explain each step, repeat the demonstration if necessary.

4. Practice—Choose someone to demonstrate the task, test for success. Provide positive feedback. Choose people who are likely to perform the task properly. Facilitate self, peer, and trainer positive critique.

5. Summary/conclusion—Review discussions, congratulate participants, provide preview of next session.

SUMMARY

This chapter presented information for supervisors to use in developing training programs and the steps for conducting training sessions. Needs assessment is vital for identifying a training problem. Once the nature of a training problem is noted, the supervisor establishes the overall training objective to solve the problem. That objective drives training program design and development. Lesson and session plans provide guidelines for training that culminate in a testing process. The final phase of training is called *reinforcement*, in which the supervisor works with newly trained individuals for a period of time to habituate the skills that were learned during the training sessions.

... In the Real World (Continued)

It has been about a year now, and despite your less-than-warm welcome and shoddy training, you have become one of the best reservation agents in the center. You know everyone in the office, and Fran, as it turns out, is kind of a nice person in her own way.

Because of your performance as an agent, Fran has decided to promote you to a supervisor position. Now you are the one standing behind five agents with your headset on and listening to their conversations. Fortunately, as an agent, you continued to take notes whenever a new situation occurred, and now you have all the information required to be an effective agent written down. You decide to compile your notes into a training manual in your spare time. When your first new agent is assigned, you introduce her to the others in your unit and escort her to a desktop in an alcove to review your manual. You ask her to jot down any questions and break away from your unit every 20 minutes or so to answer them for her. At the same time, you make mental notes on how to revise your manual. After a short period of time, you invite the new hire to shadow one of your agents, while referring to the "screen-captures" in the manual. You decide not to assign her to watch your "best" agent; instead you choose one who is patient, personable, and likes to show others how to do the job. You continue this process of read and ask, watch and ask, for two days. The new hire now feels comfortable with the basics of the agent's job. Instead of just assigning her to a terminal, you let her work on the training agent's terminal while that agent coaches her. After two days of this, the new agent tells you she is ready to fly "solo." You congratulate her for her progress and assign her to a terminal. You choose to avoid hanging over her shoulder, but instead opt to just be close enough to assist when she asks.

As time passes, you have the best work unit in the center. Some of your agents have been promoted to supervisor positions. Employee turnover in your unit is the lowest in the office. When a position becomes open in your area, experienced agents ask to work with you. Your reservation closings and revenue volumes are at an all-time high.

One day, Fran sits down with you during a coffee break and asks, "What's going on in your work unit? You are blowing the other units out of the water!" You reply, "No big thing, I just put together a nice little training program to put my guys on the right track." She tells you, "You know, the big guys are convinced that I should have an assistant manager. Are you interested in the job?"

QUESTIONS FOR DISCUSSION

1. Usually the training department in an organization is the first to go when financial times get tough. Is this a wise decision? Why or why not?

2. Sometimes a general manager will respond to poor scores on a guest service index with a mandate for new training. Would you do this or would you want more information first? If so, what would you want to know?

3. It is no secret that there is a labor crisis in the hospitality industry as well as certain other service sectors. Could training play a role in lessening the crisis? How?

4. Most operations managers think that training is a waste of money. How might you convince them otherwise?

MINI-CASE

You are a food and beverage supervisor for a large resort hotel. You have just been transferred from one of the dining rooms to one of the cocktail lounges. The beverage manager tells you that there have been numerous complaints about how long it takes to get drink orders and check totals. He tells you to set up a training program to fix the problem.

You start working in the lounge and find that there is only one point-of-sale (POS) terminal for servers to ring in orders and total checks. As far as you can tell, the servers seem to comply with the standards for service and are frustrated while waiting in line to enter their orders. You set up a meeting with the beverage manager.

You explain that you have conducted a needs analysis and there is no learning gap, thus no training need. You continue to explain that there is a resource problem (POS hardware shortage) and a systems problem (a breakdown in order placement). He replies that a new system has been ordered anyway and that additional terminals will be installed next week. He assures you that the single precheck terminal will be replaced with three machines as part of the new system.

Question:

Do you have a training situation at this point? How will you proceed with the training?

Hint:

This would be a skills training project.

KEY TERMS

Competence	Knowledge	Skills	Training
Feedback			

CHAPTER QUIZ

1.	The supervisor's manager is primarily responsible for staff training.	**T**	**F**
2.	A needs assessment is used to determine a learning gap.	**T**	**F**
3.	A learning gap demonstrates a training need.	**T**	**F**
4.	The person with the best technical skills will be the best trainer.	**T**	**F**
5.	On-the-job training requires no prior planning.	**T**	**F**
6.	Classroom training is never used in the workplace.	**T**	**F**
7.	All training is designed to give a worker actual skills.	**T**	**F**
8.	The training process is over when the training program ends.	**T**	**F**
9.	For some positions, training is a waste of time and money.	**T**	**F**
10.	Vestibule training takes place at the actual work site.	**T**	**F**

ENDNOTE

1. Robert H. Stowers, "Top Ten Tips in Teaching Communication to Executive MBA Students," *Business Communication Quarterly* 65, no. 3 (September 2002): 65.

CHAPTER SEVEN

Complaints, Grievances, and Problem Employees

OBJECTIVES

At the end of this chapter, readers will be able to:

1. Understand the role of the supervisor with regard to handling complaints and grievances.
2. Define the terms *grievance, complaint, symptom,* and *problem.*
3. Recognize the importance of listening to and acting on complaints.
4. Identify real problems after analysis of a set of symptoms.
5. Recognize the difference between a problem employee and an employee with a problem.

In the Real World . . .

You work for an events management company. You and a coworker from your department decide to take a break in the office cafeteria. You see a few people you know from other departments, so you and your friend join them. They are in the midst of a typical gripe session, and the conversation sounds something like this:

"You know, I hear that the firm across town is paying 10 percent more for the same job than I get here." "Yeah, but I hear they work you to death." "Can't be much worse than here; I haven't had a day off in two weeks." "Well, if it didn't take forever to get some replacements around here . . . I think HR is permanently on vacation." "Forget HR, my department is the place that really sucks. No resources, bad supervision, in-fighting, and whatever." "Well, in my department, only the manager's 'boys' get the goodies." "My manager tries real hard, but she claims the execs won't pay attention to her." "That's a bunch of crap. There seems to be plenty to go around when it comes time for your manager's bonus."

Finally, your silence is noticeable to the group. Someone says, "So how about you guys, I suppose you both work in wonderland." You say, "Oh no, we have our problems. Some things get fixed and others don't. But at least our management team is there to listen." One person in the group mentions, "Yeah, your managers do have pretty good reps around here. Maybe we should all transfer to your department." (To be continued)

This chapter addresses the role of managers and supervisors in handling worker complaints and grievances. In the last chapter, we mentioned that individuals sometimes prefer to avoid confrontation and conflict. We stated in a previous chapter that conflict avoidance was one reason managers communicate through memos even though verbal interaction would be more effective. The same conflict avoidance motivation may apply to the way some managers react when faced with complaints or grievances. Some managers delegate these situations upward to higher levels of the organization. This is both a mistake and a breach of responsibility. The manager is responsible for the organizational welfare of his workers. When a manager does not fulfill the duty of handling complaints, he is not acting in accordance with this responsibility. By delegating complaints and grievances upward, the manager becomes disempowered and loses the respect of the workers. Here is an illustration of this concept.

> Bob is a department manager at an exclusive resort. He has 14 people working in his department. Bob is a nice guy. The workers in his department like him. Mr. Bizri is Bob's boss. When new policies or directives are put in place, Bob tells the staff that Mr. Bizri made the rules. When workers complain about company benefits or problems with their paychecks, Bob refers them to Mr. Bizri or the company payroll clerk. When two or more workers have a conflict, Bob tries to smooth things over by saying, "Come on guys, let's just work together." The workers have a tendency to go to Mr. Bizri with their problems, instead of talking to Bob. While everyone likes Bob, they don't seem to respect him as a manager.
>
> What factors have caused the staff to lack respect for Bob as a manager?

Experienced managers realize that it is more important to be admired and respected than to be liked by the workers. In most operations departments, the workers deal directly with the customers. Managers should realize that the services provided to the workers reflect on the services provided by the workers to the customers. The role of manager is to provide service-based support to the workers.

EMPLOYEE RELATIONS TERMINOLOGY

Grievance—A complaint received from a worker about perceived unfair treatment in the organization.

Terminology used in dealing with employee relations problems seems similar and vague to some observers. The word **grievance** is often used synonymously with the word *complaint*. All grievances are complaints. However, not all complaints are grievances. A grievance is a complaint with regard to the perception that a work-related right or privilege has been violated. The key word here is perception. A grievance is merely an allegation of unfair treatment. Whether the violation actually took place depends on the outcome of an investigation. The important concept is that a person who files a grievance perceives a violation of a right or privilege. Therefore, the manager must pay attention to the worker. The manager should listen to the worker's situation and take the appropriate steps to identify the facts. After the fact-finding activities are completed, the manager should follow up with the worker and make the appropriate decision.

Complaint—The communication of dissatisfaction with a situation.

A **complaint** may be applied to just about any topic. An individual may complain whenever there is a perception of dissatisfaction concerning any perceived unfavorable experience. This is different than a grievance, which is a specific allegation that a right or a privilege of the employee has been violated. For instance, a worker who claims that the food in the employee cafeteria is disgusting is certainly complaining. But the nature of this complaint is not a grievance. On the other hand, a worker who complains that a supervisor is engaging in harassing behavior is lodging a grievance

Symptom—An observable fact in the environment that may be used to diagnose a problem.

Problem—A negative gap between standards for performance and actual performance.

Most complaints are **symptoms** of underlying **problems.** For instance, a worker remarks that the food in the employee cafeteria is disgusting. Upon further questioning, the manager determines that the real problem is that the cafeteria served rice three times this week and the employee doesn't like rice. Therefore, the problem isn't the quality of the food; rather, it is lack of a variety of food items. This is a very different problem. The solution is probably easy. Perhaps the cafeteria manager may be persuaded to alternate starches between rice and potatoes every other day.

Identifying real problems requires sifting through complaints, which articulate symptoms of a problem. Once the problem is identified, the solution is usually easily established. Remember, the most difficult aspect to problem solving is identifying the real problem.

WORK-RELATED ISSUES

Work-related issues are those topics specifically associated with the organization, its customers, and its workers. Any issue outside this realm is not a work-related issue. Issues that are not work related are beyond the scope of the manager's expertise; therefore, managers are encouraged to refrain from discussing these issues. Examples of these issues are: politics, religion, and certain aspects related to personal problems and domestic relationships.

These and other personal topics are beyond the scope of managerial discussion. Of course, there are times when personal problems affect work performance. In these cases the manager must differentiate between work-related aspects and those best left for mental health and other therapeutic practitioners.

THE IRATE COMPLAINER

There are times when workers will lodge complaints while in a state of emotional upset. At times the complaining worker may be agitated or angry. This presents a dilemma for the manager, who may be dealing with a worker who is acting in an insubordinate manner. While insubordination may be inappropriate, experienced managers realize the need to defuse emotion from the situation before proceeding with any action. Also, managers should consider the circumstances surrounding the worker's behavior.

OPEN DOOR POLICIES

Open door policy— The availability of the supervisors to discuss concerns of the workers within an organization.

Some managers feel uncomfortable with open door policies. An **open door policy** permits employees to discuss their concerns with a person other than the supervisor. This is an advisable practice, since there are situations in which employees may feel uncomfortable discussing certain issues directly with the supervisor. It is suggested that upper-level managers and human resources people ask the worker if the problem was discussed with the supervisor. If the answer is no, the reason should be determined. In some cases it would be appropriate for the manager to encourage the employee to discuss the situation with the immediate supervisor. However, in other cases this would be inappropriate, and the manager hearing the complaint should choose an alternative intervention. In either case, the situation should be discussed with the direct supervisor at some point in time.

THE IMMEDIATE SUPERVISOR

The most important individual in the professional life of a worker is the immediate supervisor. The immediate supervisor should be a coach, trainer, mentor, and supporter of the workers. Some supervisors abdicate their responsibilities. This results in loss of influence for the supervisor. Managers and supervisors who fail to listen to complaints and grievances from workers are providing opportunities for other people to represent the interests of the workers. In organizations where workers do not feel they are being heard, outside parties, such as labor unions, are sometimes sought to represent them.

So far, we have discussed complaints and grievances lodged by employees with supervisors. As we indicated, smart supervisors view the practice of listening to these as opportunities to learn about the workers and to become heroes in those cases in which they are able to solve employee problems. It is important to note, however, that there is a difference between an employee with a problem and a "problem employee." In the first case there is a perceived situation of adversity. In the latter, the individual is becoming a liability to the performance of the organization through destructive behaviors.

DEALING WITH PROBLEM EMPLOYEES

Problem employees— Individuals employed by an organization who exhibit chronic behaviors deemed to be destructive to the performance of a work unit.

KSAAs—Knowledge, skills, attitudes, and abilities to perform the tasks, duties, and responsibilities of a position within an organization in a productive manner.

How is it that **problem employees** exist in organizations? This is an apparently simple question requiring a somewhat complicated answer. Despite efforts to recruit and select individuals who are potential productive members of an organization, the process is never foolproof. Human resources practitioners are in the business of identifying those individuals who possess the appropriate knowledge, skills, attitudes, and abilities (**KSAAs**) for an open position.

Thus, some people who are hired and even complete probationary periods do become problem employees, not because of a deficiency in KSAAs, but due to some form of mental "baggage" that surfaces during the employment tenure. In these cases there are emotional or psychological factors that cause certain individuals to be unable to assimilate to a position within the organization. In these cases, the cause of the problem is beyond our area of expertise as managers, and those individuals will eventually end up being "managed out" of the organization, as we will discuss in the next chapter. There are, however, other factors that may contribute to the development of a problem employee that may not be within her personal domain.

In some cases jobs are poorly designed due to improper or nonexistent job analysis activities. This will cause unnecessary stress for workers, which could cause them to behave in destructive ways. Absence of clarity in the workplace could be another factor contributing to problem workers. It is the

purpose of documents such as job descriptions and job specifications to articulate abilities as well as specific tasks, duties, and responsibilities for each position. The absence of these documents may result in a level of ambiguity that
may be intolerable for certain individuals, which could result in destructive
workplace behaviors. Also, in the event that these documents do not exist, it
would be impossible to have clearly defined policies, standards, procedures,
and benchmarks for performance, which would further agitate a person with
a low tolerance for ambiguity. As discussed in the previous chapter, insuffi-
cient skills and knowledge training would contribute to increased work stress,
resulting in undesirable behaviors.

All of these issues, of course, are the responsibility of the managers
within the organization. This makes it difficult to legitimately find fault with
adverse workplace behaviors. Knowledgeable managers will "put their own
house in order" before finding fault with unproductive employees.

Regardless of cause, there are a few generic prototypes of problem employees worth mentioning. Problem employees display behaviors that range
from passive-aggressive to truly problematic.

One category of problem employee is known as "the slacker." This one is
moving at half the pace of everyone else, takes more breaks, shows up late,
leaves early, and always seems to have a headache or a doctor's appointment.
When this person looks for a partner, everyone runs in the other direction.
Also, this person is always totally unaware of what his peers think of him (he
thinks they actually like him). The reason for this is that this type of individual is usually in possession of pseudo or total narcissistic tendencies.

Another generic type of problem employee is often heard saying things
like, "It's too hot, it's unfair, it's too hard, everyone picks on me, my schedule
stinks, the cafeteria is awful, the guests are obnoxious, my feet hurt, my uniform is too tight, my manager hates me, my paycheck is always wrong, nobody told me, my station is too small, this computer doesn't work." By now
you may have guessed that this person is known as "the whiner." Most people

---

HOSPITALITY TIPS & CLIPS *No Way, You Haven't Hired a Slacker, Have You?*

Have you hired a slacker? Following are the top 10 rules of slackers. It might help you to understand such employees better if you understand their rules.

1. If something is worth doing, let someone else do it.
2. If you can't succeed, just forget it.
3. I'm a firm believer in what's mine is mine and what's yours is mine, too.
4. Deadlines are a waste of my time.
5. I'll continue to make excuses and not be a team player.
6. I'll always find a reason for my failures because surely they are not my fault.
7. I don't give a darn what my family, friends, and coworkers think of me. It's their problem, not mine!
8. I'll spend many hours explaining my problems and inadequacies to anyone who will listen.
9. I receive satisfaction by being a difficult person to deal with.
10. I don't need to improve my knowledge about my job.

Source: Hospitality News. "No Way, You Haven't Hired a Slacker Have You?" *Hospitality News* (June–July 2002): p. 10. Courtesy of *Hospitality News*.

---

in this category have a persistent need for attention, either in the form of commiseration, special treatment, or even blank stares.

On the other hand, "the arguer" is interested in forcing people into admitting she is right, no matter what the issue. This person always sees things differently than everyone else. If you say it is black, she says it is white. You think you are doing a favor for this person and she complains. This person has a negative opinion about everything and everyone. The only person who agrees with the arguer is herself. Actually, similar to the whiner, the arguer is seeking attention, but wants it only in the form of validation of her opinions. Some individuals who are labeled as arguers are just people who sort information in terms of differences, as opposed to the majority of the population who sort things in terms of similarities. Show three coins (a quarter, a dime, and a nickel) to an arguer, for instance, and he will likely note that they are different sizes, different denominations, with different presidents on each face. Most other individuals would have the tendency to say they are all silver, they are all money, and they are all forms of loose change. Is there a place for the arguer in your organization?

Actually there are places in organizations for all the categories of problem employees except the slacker. The slacker simply must be managed into a different career with any organization other than your own. Arguers, on the other hand, are great in positions that require an eye for discrepancies. They are good auditors, accountants, risk managers, inspectors, and repair personnel. Whiners are perfect for using test products. If they can't find anything to complain about, it is likely your customers won't find anything to complain about. Also, since whiners are motivated by attention, they may be converted to the silent majority by withholding attention on whining behaviors and placing them in the "spotlight" for productive behaviors.

SUMMARY

This chapter has provided information for supervisors to effectively deal with negative conflict in the workplace. As we will discover in later chapters, conflict is not always a bad situation. However, the type of conflict discussed in this chapter has to do with perceived unfairness, which is never appropriate in an organization. We determined that complaints and grievances are not the same, but both may be symptoms of some problem. This took us to discussion of analyzing symptoms in an effort to identify and solve real problems. As we discussed in earlier chapters, the key to problem resolution is effective listening skills on the part of the supervisor. We also discovered that there is a distinct difference between employees with problems and problem employees. We concluded this chapter with discussion concerning the cause, identification, and possible corrective actions for these individuals.

... *In the Real World* (*Continued*)

Later that same day, one of the people who were sitting at the table stops by your department to see you. She says, "You know, I really like those guys as friends. But most of them are total slackers and losers. I really would like to see if there are opportunities to transfer to your department." You say, "I've seen your work, you do a great job. I hear that someone here is going to be promoted out of the department soon. Her job is very similar to the one you do now. Come on, I'll introduce you to the department director."

QUESTIONS FOR DISCUSSION

1. Some individuals would contend that the information presented in this chapter is a waste of time by saying that all these individuals should just be replaced with hard-working, quiet individuals who just take what life has to give them without complaining. Is this a good idea? Why or why not?

2. What should you do when a person complains to you about something that is totally beyond your power to fix? Is there a correct way to handle this? Is there an incorrect way to handle this?

3. If "attitude" is one of the KSAAs that we look for in hiring people, why do we end up with some individuals who later display bad attitudes?

MINI-CASE

You are a human resources practitioner for an events management firm. You know that one of the departments has been poorly run for about two years. The manager of that department has recently been replaced with an individual who is charged with turning the unit around to a productive working area. You have been warned that such an intervention will create negative "ripples" among some of the existing staff members, who are accustomed to engaging in unproductive behaviors. It is the stated intention of the new manager to "weed out" certain poor performers.

Sure enough, the employees are starting to run to you with complaints and grievances about how the new manager is treating them.

Question:

How do you handle these?

Hint:

Refusing to listen to them is not an option.

 KEY TERMS

Complaint	Open door policy	Problem	Symptom
Grievance	Problem	employee	
KSAAs			

CHAPTER QUIZ

1. It is better for a supervisor to be respected than to be liked.   **T**   **F**
2. All grievances are complaints.   **T**   **F**
3. If a person complains a lot, the supervisor should not listen to him/her.   **T**   **F**
4. Most problems are easily identifiable through complaints.   **T**   **F**
5. All complaints are symptoms of a problem.   **T**   **F**
6. Once a problem is identified, it is usually pretty easy to solve.   **T**   **F**
7. Supervisors should blame their bosses for policy decisions.   **T**   **F**
8. A manager who is accessible to the staff has an open door policy.   **T**   **F**
9. There is no need to take action after a person lodges a grievance.   **T**   **F**
10. Smart supervisors listen closely to the nature of a complaint.   **T**   **F**

CHAPTER EIGHT

Coaching, Counseling, Discipline, and the Law

OBJECTIVES

At the end of this chapter, readers will be able to:

1. Identify the components of performance.
2. Recognize the difference between counseling and discipline.
3. Understand criteria for progressive discipline.
4. Recognize the role of the immediate supervisor in counseling and discipline issues.
5. Recognize the legal rights of individuals when it comes to disciplinary situations.

In the Real World . . .

You are an assistant beverage manager on a cruise ship. You are responsible for all of the bartenders, cocktail servers, and barbacks on board the ship. Like most cruise lines, your vessel flies a foreign flag, and your employees are contracted from countries outside the United States. A contracted employee who fails to perform aboard most ships would simply be disembarked at the next port. However, your cruise line has a policy of adhering to human resources policies in accordance with U.S. federal law and common management standards within that country. Therefore, you practice coaching, counseling, and progressive discipline with the members of the staff.

On this trip you have a few new cocktail servers. The rest of the staff has been thoroughly trained. One of the new cocktail servers seems to be having trouble doing her job. Also, you have been watching one of the veteran bartenders for quite awhile and you suspect she is stealing liquor. Finally, at the beginning of this 10-day trip, a female passenger lodged a complaint with the purser that another bartender had treated her in a rude manner, but wasn't very specific with exactly what he said or did to her.

You decide that you will resolve each of these matters by the end of this trip. (To be continued)

Organizations are complex entities with large numbers of people as members of the staff. The purpose of every worker is to contribute to the mission of the company by serving the customers according to prescribed standards. Managers provide the main source of support for the workers in an organization. The workers are the customers of the managers. The managers are responsible for training, communicating expectations, observing behaviors, evaluating performance, and providing feedback to the workers. Also, managers have record-keeping responsibilities for documenting training and evaluations of worker performance.[1]

Some managers believe that training, counseling, and discipline are the responsibilities of the human resources department. The opposite is true. Human resources professionals merely assist managers with these tasks.[2] The ultimate responsibility is within the domain of the immediate supervisor or manager.

This chapter provides a practical approach to the practice of counseling and discipline. The key component to effective counseling and discipline is clear, concise, and timely communication with workers. Many managers avoid criticizing performance because they don't want to participate in negative interactions. By remaining silent, managers are actually doing harm to the workers. When the supervisor fails to challenge undesired behaviors, the worker assumes that the behavior is condoned or acceptable. The worker will continue the behavior in the absence of feedback. The supervisor will eventually reach a point of intolerance toward the behavior. At this point, the manager considers replacing the worker due to repeated performance problems. In actuality, the manager contributed to the repeat behaviors by not redirecting the worker on the first or second occurrence. Small problems left unattended often develop into major situations that hamper performance. Managers should address the little problems before they develop into major issues.

EXPECTATIONS

Goals—The targets for performance in an organization; objectives.
Standards—The expectations for performance in an organization.
Procedures—The listing of tasks that result in meeting standards for performance.

Before there can be any discussion of discipline or counseling, the manager must clarify the **goals** for behavior in the organization. The goals should be measurable, achievable, specific, objective, and somewhat challenging. These types of goals are sometimes referred to as **standards.** For each performance standard, there should be a **procedure** for attaining the standard. The standards and procedures should be clearly communicated. Managers must provide training to deliver the knowledge and skills required to perform the procedures in ways that meet the established standards. The standards and procedures, along with training objectives, comprise the expectations for performance in the organization.

OBSERVED BEHAVIOR

Managers spend a good deal of time observing the behaviors of workers. These observations of actual performance should be compared to the expectations or standards for performance. The important consideration is that the behaviors are the focus of observation. Some managers look beyond actual behaviors into personalities, attitudes, and other subjective criteria. Behavior is purely objective; it either happens or it doesn't. If a manager perceives an attitude problem, the manager should identify specific behaviors that indicate that the worker is not meeting expectations. For instance, a worker may speak loudly to customers, continually frown, fail to assist coworkers when asked, and use profanity excessively in the presence of others. These behaviors would not meet the standards for most organizations. Some managers would witness these behaviors and say that the worker has a "bad attitude." Which is more specific—the behaviors or a "bad attitude"? Managers should describe only behaviors and refrain from judgmental comments when describing performance.

HOSPITALITY TIPS & CLIPS *Wasting Time on the Job*

There are a host of reasons why employees waste time. Following are the most common time wasters that should be addressed by management:

- Personal phone calls
- Long lunch hours or breaks (a few minutes here and there add up over the course of a week)
- Time spent visiting with coworkers
- Handling personal and family problems on company time

- Coming in late and leaving early
- Overuse of restrooms
- Lack of focus on customers
- Not improving job performance (requiring repeated training)
- Failing to focus on work

Source: "Wasting Time on the Job." *Hospitality News* (August 2002): p. 15. Courtesy of *Hospitality News.*

EVALUATION

When managers compare actual performance (behaviors) with standards they are evaluating performance. Performance evaluations take place informally and formally. Informal performance evaluations should occur every working day. The formal appraisals are usually scheduled every few months or annually (Chapter 10 provides more thorough discussion on this). A manager spends an average of 2,000 hours per year with each worker. Yet many managers would find it difficult to account for 200 hours of performance observations over the course of a year.[3]

The Critical Incident Method

Critical incident method—A method for recording and recalling observable behaviors that are important aspects of worker performance.

One technique for tracking performance observations is called the **critical incident method.** This method involves jotting down notes concerning critical incidents of performance. Critical means an event that is noteworthy. Managers may take brief notes of critical performance observations as they make their rounds in the operation. It takes only a few minutes to jot down some brief phrases in a notebook or pad. When the manager returns to the office, the notes may be placed in separate files for each worker. At the end of the year, the notes may be reviewed and used to conduct a formal performance appraisal. Here is an example of the critical incident technique:

> Liz is the manager of a department at an exclusive resort. She has a large department with 60 workers. There are two assistant managers and four supervisors who report to Liz. Recently, a conversation was overheard among a few of the supervisors and assistant managers in the employee cafeteria. One person said, "You won't believe the move Liz pulled on me today. We were talking and she said, 'I seem to remember you telling me you would have the inventory control system completed by 8:30 on September 10. Is it ready?' She must have a photographic memory." Another person chimed in, "Last week she discussed my annual review. She cited dates and times of specific performance scenarios going back to last October. I swear she must be videotaping me or something."

In the story above, the workers are obviously impressed with the fact that Liz, the manager, seems to recall every promised due date and every important performance scenario from the past year. Liz does not have a photographic memory. And she is not recording videotapes of her workers. Liz simply practices the critical incident method of recording observations. For instance, when a worker promises to deliver a project or report at a future date, Liz will jot a note after the worker leaves the office. Liz places the note in a trace file for reference on the due date. Each day, Liz checks the trace file for that date to see what projects are due.

When it comes to formal performance appraisals, Liz realizes that she spends 2,000 hours per year with each worker. Liz also knows that she cannot accurately recall every incident over that time period for every worker. So, Liz jots notes in her daytimer or on a small pad as she makes her daily rounds. She then takes 5 or 10 minutes of office time each day to place the notes in a file folder for each worker. When the time comes for a performance review, Liz simply pulls the file and reviews her notes. This provides Liz with a snapshot of critical incidents for the entire year. The notes jog her memory of what she has observed over a long period of time.

The critical incident method provides managers with a tool for recording and reviewing performance scenarios.[4] Managers who use this method are perceived by workers to be fair and objective in their evaluations of workers' behavior. The critical incident method takes very little time to practice and yields huge benefits in terms of fair, uniform, and consistent reviews of performance. Therefore, the method is both efficient and effective.

COACHING

Coaching—Working with individuals to progressively develop their skills and habits.

When workers are in training, the manager should act as a coach. When in **coaching** mode, the manager watches behaviors and focuses on the things that were done almost right.[5] For instance, a worker is practicing the standards for telephone etiquette. The worker answers the phone and fails to state his name. The manager who is coaching the worker might tell him that the phone was answered promptly, that the appropriate salutation was used, and that the worker sounded pleasant when answering. All of these are things the worker did right. Now, the manager might say, "Do it exactly like you did it before, but this time, tell the caller who you are." This is an example of coaching. When a worker is in learning mode, the manager wants to provide encouragement. Therefore, the manager tells the worker what was done right and coaches the worker to do the task a little better. Finally, the worker will perform the task perfectly.

COUNSELING

Counseling— Providing advice for the welfare of an individual.

Counseling is similar to coaching, in that the manager provides the worker with the benefit of doubt that the worker may not have clearly understood the expectation. Counseling is a technique for redirecting behavior.[6] A counseling

session should occur as soon as possible after the incident. However, counseling should always be done in a private area away from other workers. When a manager counsels a worker, the manager should cite the specific behavior of the worker. Let's consider a scenario in which a manager has asked an employee to step into a private office for a discussion. Once inside the office, the manager says, "I noticed you answered the phone on two occasions this morning after the phone rang more than three times. Do you recall these incidents?" The worker proceeds to explain or provide excuses for the behavior. The manager listens for a reasonable period of time and responds, "I realize that it gets hectic from time to time. However, the standard is to answer the phone within three rings. We must meet the standard. If you find that circumstances cause us to not meet the standard, ask for help from me or a coworker. We cannot jeopardize our standards. Do you understand the importance of this issue? Do you agree that you will do what is necessary to meet the standard? Good. I'm here to help."

In the above scenario, the manager conducted the conversation in a private area. She gave the worker an opportunity to explain the action. She then reinforced the standard and provided assistance for the worker to meet the standard. The manager encouraged the worker to respond with agreement to the solution, acceptance of responsibility, and demonstrated understanding of the issue. These are ingredients of a constructive counseling session.

HOSPITALITY TIPS & CLIPS *Defusing an Angry Employee*

When an angry employee confronts you, you must respond—but not in kind. You need to carefully control your response and work to disarm this person who is attempting to intimidate you. Here are some suggestions:

- **Don't respond impulsively.** This is a natural reaction: to lash out or defend yourself or your position. Doing so rarely contributes to a positive outcome. Instead, think carefully and respond deliberately. Ask yourself, "Will what I'm about to say help or hurt the situation?"
- **Don't take it personally.** This is hard to do, but rarely are people attacking you personally. There is usually some more complicated reason behind their harsh words, and your task is to find out what their motivation is all about.
- **Put yourself in the other person's place.** This will help you avoid taking her words

personally and responding impulsively. Hostility often arises out of anxiety, exhaustion, frustration, or overwork. Don't make excuses for bad behavior, but understanding the circumstances might enable you to respond more positively.
- Most important of all, **control your voice, tone, and language.** Oftentimes your voice rises to a higher pitch when you are excited or angry. That's a sure sign you are losing control, and when you realize that, it will help you control your voice and your emotions. Never respond by using foul or harsh language.

Source: "Defusing an Angry Employee." *Hospitality News* (April 2002): p. 46. Courtesy of *Hospitality News.*

DISCIPLINE

Discipline—
Redirecting behaviors to achieve the objectives of an organization.

Discipline is different from coaching and counseling. Discipline should occur when a worker knows the expected behavior and acts in a manner contrary to the expectation. Discipline should be progressive; that is, the action taken should meet with the severity of the behavior.[7] Also, future disciplinary actions should progressively meet with repetitive occurrences. There are two behaviors that warrant discipline. The first is poor performance, which is the failure to meet performance standards. When a worker knows the expectations for performance and willfully fails to perform to standards, discipline may be the appropriate response.[8] The second issue is misconduct, which involves violations of policy or procedure. In some misconduct instances, immediate **discharge** is warranted. These incidents are called **gross misconduct.** Other misconduct issues may warrant warnings to change behavior. Progressive action will result from reoccurrence. Finally, discharge may be appropriate if the worker does not change behavior.[9]

Discharge—
Involuntary separation from an organization.

Gross misconduct—A violation of the rules for behavior in an organization that warrants immediate employee discharge.

There are a few factors to consider with regard to disciplinary actions. The key factor is to administer discipline in a fashion that is perceived by the workers as fair, uniform, and consistent. Suggestions are listed below to assist managers with providing discipline that meets these criteria:

- Gather and weigh the facts concerning the incident.
- Decide what action to take depending on the severity of the incident.
- Interview the worker by focusing on the behaviors (not the worker as a person).
- Give the worker a chance to explain.
- Evaluate the worker's explanation. If more facts are required, establish a time for a second meeting.
- Notify the worker of the action, what future actions will be taken if behaviors occur again, and the rationale for the action taken.
- Document the incident, the investigation of facts, the interview with the worker, the action taken, and progressive future actions (if appropriate).
- Ensure that this worker is treated the same as all other workers under similar circumstances.
- Provide for multiple-party reviews and an appeal process for workers within the organization.

LEGAL RIGHTS OF EMPLOYEES

One of the guiding principles for the suggestions listed above is the legal environment pertaining to employment relationships. There are legal aspects involved in every term, condition, right, and privilege of employment. Thus, management activities to include hiring, promoting, training, transferring, and discharge are subject to compliance with state and federal antidiscrimination laws.

Historically, in the United States individuals were discriminated against in employment, as well as in other societal practices. To right these social wrongs, civil rights laws were legislated to ban discrimination as early as the 1860s. While these laws are still invoked in current-day court cases, the landmark civil rights legislation is the Civil Rights Act (CRA) of 1964, as amended in 1972 and reamended in 1991. The CRA was created and written by Congress, which makes this law a federal statute, part of a body of written law known as "statutory law." Both statutory (written) law and tort or common (judge-made) law apply to employment relationships. For most states in the country there are state statutes that replicate and expand upon those provided at the federal level. Thus, human resources practitioners must be familiar with the laws for the country as well as those that apply in the state in which the service enterprise is doing business. The section of the CRA that pertains to employment relationships is referred to as Title VII. The coverage of the CRA includes protection from discrimination based on race, sex, color, national origin, and religion. Collectively, people who are afforded coverage under any of these categories are referred to as "protected class" individuals. Interestingly, when the CRA was created, a definition for what constituted illegal discrimination was not included.

In a landmark case known as *Griggs vs. Duke Power*, the U.S. Supreme Court defined four theories of discrimination. The first theory was known as Perpetuation, in which it became illegal to continue (perpetuate) past discriminatory practices. Another theory is called Disparate Treatment, which precludes any form of illegal intentional discrimination against a person who is a member of a protected class. A third theory is similar to this but protects groups of individuals within any specific protected class from even unintentional discrimination and is known as Disparate Impact. A final theory underlies

such laws as the Americans with Disabilities Act (ADA), and is known as Accommodations, in which employers must "accommodate" employees with special needs in a reasonable manner. All of these theories may have implications for disciplinary actions taken by employers against employees; however, the area of specific interest for this topic is the theory of Disparate Treatment.

In order for a person to lodge a claim of Disparate Treatment, he must demonstrate that an adverse decision was made toward him, that the decision was intentionally discriminatory, and that he incurred harm (suffering) resulting from the decision. To demonstrate this, the burden of proof is placed upon the individual seeking to make a claim of Disparate Treatment or any type of discrimination. In actual practice, all an employee really has to do is to march down to the local Equal Employment Opportunity Commission (EEOC) office and claim that he was fired, which made him lose money, and that the employer was intentionally discriminating against him because of his protected class status (race, sex, color, religion, national origin). This simple gesture satisfies an employee's (now referred to as the complainant) burden of proof within the law. The EEOC will listen to the person's complaint and run through a checklist of potential areas of discrimination. This process takes less than one hour. Next, the EEOC will issue a Notice of Finding of Fact to the employer, now officially known as the respondent in the eyes of the law. The employer now incurs the burden of proof to demonstrate that it did not discriminate. This process will likely take more than 100 hours of work to provide sufficient documentation to support the employer's actions. If the employer does not satisfy the EEOC with a presentation of facts, informal and formal hearings will ensue, and ultimately the issue may be taken to federal district court. It is important to note that the CRA (1964–1991) is not the only statute that is applicable to employment relationships. There are many others that require varying activities for compliance.

Other than the ethical duty to do the right thing, employers and all agents for employers (managers and supervisors) possess the legal duty to comply with state and federal laws. Because of the burden of proof that is placed on the employer in the event of a legal complaint, managers must be appropriately versed in employment law issues (a topic for a human resources management course or training program) and act in accordance with those laws. However, managers also have the responsibility of accomplishing the objectives of the organization through the activities of others. Attorneys are not managers and managers are not attorneys. This is why human resources practitioners need to be knowledgeable in both disciplines of management and employment law, which again is a topic for that respective program.

SUMMARY

It is important to note that coaching, counseling, and discipline are feedback processes concerning the performance of employees. Employees expect feedback. It is the responsibility of the manager to provide appropriate feedback concerning workers' behavior. The important aspect of counseling and discipline is the perception of the workers that the manager works fairly, uniformly, and consistently. Discipline is not necessarily a punitive process.

Instead, it is a form of feedback that provides workers with opportunities to redirect behaviors to meet expectations of the organization. Finally, all decisions regarding rights, privileges, and responsibilities within the employment relationship must be legally sound.

...In the Real World (Continued)

You've decided to start with the new cocktail server. Although she managed to pass her training tests, you notice a few problems with her service after some careful observation. For one thing, she has trouble balancing her trays and sometimes topples items. You spend some time with her in a closed outlet to show her how to place items on the tray, balance the tray during her walk to a table, and remove the items from the tray. To avoid any further breakage, you use plastic containers containing water. After a while she gets the hang of tray-handling skills. The next thing you work on is garnishes. The ship serves a number of tropical cocktails requiring various garnishes. You show her a couple of easy tricks for remembering each garnish, and she soon gets that down pat. The final thing you notice is that she is mixing up her drink order abbreviations, which is causing her to mis-ring items from her order pad, which results in waste. You review those with her by turning the abbreviations into little memory games. In a couple of days, the cocktail server is almost as good as her veteran peers. She is thankful for the time you spent coaching her.

Meanwhile, you review the purser's log of the rudeness incident with the bartender. You identify the name of the complaining passenger and visit her to apologize for the incident and to get some specific information. The passenger tells you, "Oh, I am sure it was a misunderstanding, but I think the bartender could have been nicer to me." You then spend some time with the bartender to listen to his side of the story. The two stories match, and you realize he could have done a better job with the passenger. You counsel him on what to do with similar incidents in the future and document your session with a note to file.

As for your theft suspect, she certainly does nothing out of the ordinary when you are watching her work. You learn from the purser that there is an available cabin on board and ask the food and beverage director to provide you with a "mystery shopper." This person embarks at the next port to visit your bartender during her working hours. The shopper notices that each time the bartender makes a straight-up martini, she holds the shaker very low behind the bar and continues to pour the gin into a juice container on the glass rack just next to where she is holding the shaker. By the end of the shift, she has an almost full juice container of top-shelf gin that she removes from the bar in a gym bag and takes to her quarters. Armed with the shopper's report, you arrange for ship security personnel to conduct a "bag check" with the bartender as she is entering her quarters. Sure enough, the juice container that is removed from her bag is nearly full of gin. This is gross misconduct—the possession of contraband—as stated in your policy manual and grounds for immediate dismissal. This is a matter of discipline and you arrange for this person to disembark at the next port of call.

QUESTIONS FOR DISCUSSION

1. Some managers say you really know how to deal with people when they thank you for firing them! How can this be?

2. Some new managers are very quick to fire nonperformers. Is this a mistake? Why or why not?

3. Some books tell you to make verbal warnings before written warnings. Is there really any such thing (if the manager is smart) as a warning that is not written down? Why?

MINI-CASE

You are a front office manager at a medium-size branded hotel. The hotel follows corporate standards of procedure to the letter. Your best front desk agent was notified last week that he was selected for the manager-in-training (MIT) program by the corporation upon his graduation from school this semester. This news had him and you quite stoked, as he really wants a management career with this chain.

One night is extremely busy at the front desk with long check-in lines. Your "star agent" has picked up his bank from the general cashier, placed it into the terminal drawer, and started checking in guests. Some of the other agents see the mayhem before they pick up their banks and jump behind the desk to help with check-ins. Contrary to company policy, your star agent lets other agents use his bank. At the close of the shift, he is exactly $200 short. According to company policy, any bank discrepancy over $50 is grounds for disciplinary action. Also, an individual who has a disciplinary notice in the personnel file is ineligible to participate in the MIT program. He offers to replace the money from his own pocket. But company policy prohibits that, and even if he did, the disciplinary action would still be required. You realize that one of his coworkers ripped him off, but can't prove it. It was partly his fault because company policy prohibits giving other individuals access to your personal bank. You feel bad for this guy because this incident will ruin his opportunity to break in to management.

Question:

What are you going to do?

Hint:

There are rules and there are exceptions to rules, but exceptions include risk.

 KEY TERMS

Coaching
Counseling
Critical incident method

Discharge
Discipline
Goals

Gross misconduct
Procedures
Standards

CHAPTER QUIZ

1. Counseling is the same as discipline. **T F**
2. Coaching involves encouraging people to develop their skills. **T F**
3. Standards are expectations for performance in the workplace. **T F**
4. Discussions with employees should focus on observable behaviors. **T F**

5.	There are two issues in the workplace: performance and conduct.	**T**	**F**
6.	A person who commits an act of gross misconduct should be counseled.	**T**	**F**
7.	Progressive discipline includes warnings of future consequences.	**T**	**F**
8.	Counseling and discipline should take place in private with the worker.	**T**	**F**
9.	Procedures provide a list of steps to meet with performance standards.	**T**	**F**
10.	The human resources department does all counseling and discipline.	**T**	**F**

ENDNOTES

1. Lisa A. Dicke, "Ensuring Accountability in Human Services Contracting: Can Stewardship Theory Fill the Bill?" *American Review of Public Administration* 32, no. 4 (December 2002): 455.
2. Joe Vocino, "HR Feels Pinch of Economic Slowdown," *HR Magazine* 47, no. 11 (November 2002): 58.
3. Lillian T. Eby, "Further Investigation of Protégés' Negative Mentoring Experiences: Patterns and Outcomes," *Group & Organization Management* 27, no. 4 (December 2002): 456.
4. Ibid.
5. Marilyn E. Laiken, "Managing the Action/Reflection Polarity in the OD Classroom: A Path to Transformative Learning," *Organization Development Journal* 20, no. 3 (Fall 2002): 52.
6. Jeffrey Becker, "Discrepancies in Self/Subordinates' Perceptions of Leadership Behavior: Leader's Gender, Organizational Context, and Leader's Self-Monitoring," *Group & Organization Management* 27, no. 2 (June 2002): 226.
7. Ted Ingalls, "Is Punishment an Appropriate Option?" *Occupational Health & Safety* 71, no. 9 (September 2002): 229.
8. D.V. Tesone, *Human Resources Management for the Hospitality Industry: A Practitioner's Perspective* (Upper Saddle River, NJ, Prentice Hall, 2004).
9. John A. Rohr, "Dicey's Ghost and Administrative Law," *Administration & Society* 34, no. 1 (March 2002): 8.

CHAPTER NINE
Building Teams

OBJECTIVES

At the end of this section, readers will be able to:

1. Identify the components of effective teams.
2. Recognize the importance of hiring team players.
3. Manage conflict among team members.
4. Practice collaborative planning.

In the Real World . . .

You are the assistant manager for a restaurant that is part of a small chain of 10 stores. You are attending the annual awards conference for the chain at a beautiful resort. Once again, your restaurant has won the highest achievement award for total revenues and net profit. Many of the employees from your store are at the conference and are rightfully celebrating the victory in grand style. Tonight is the awards dinner to be held in the grand ballroom.

You are lounging at the tiki bar in the recreation area. A couple of managers from other stores buy you a drink. One of them mentions, "You guys have been winning most of the awards ever since I joined the company. What's up with that?"

You decide to tell your story. "We are not your typical restaurant," you start off saying. "For instance, we don't have bussers, host staff, or barbacks. Everyone takes care of his or her own stations and areas. The managers work the door and the floor. There is no such saying as 'it's not my job' in our store. Everyone is part of the team. The servers have stations and every one of them makes a minimum of 25 per cent of average sales. But their job is to roam the rest of the floor to see how they can assist the other guests. If one of them gets in the 'weeds' they ask for help and the floater is dispatched to them, and servers in the nearest stations also assist them. We don't take breaks during meal periods. If someone needs a break there is a floater who covers those periodically. The same is true for the income and activities of bartenders. Every person on the culinary team knows every station in the kitchen and frequently works each one. The same is true for most of the service staff; most of them have completed culinary training. That way, they can fill in for the kitchen staff when they get in the 'weeds.' Every manager knows every job in the house; you can't become a manager until you have this ability. We have twice the number of managers than a normal store. But we make so much money, we can afford the salaries, and nobody sits in an office while we are doing business. Our turnover is practically nothing, but when we do need a team member people don't interview, they audition for the job. During a person's audition time (usually one month) every team member votes on whether the person should join us. It is kind of like a fraternity or sorority; you either get "blackballed" or voted in."

The managers look at you with mouths agape: "We never heard of such a thing!" "Well," you reply, "buy me another drink and I'll tell you how things got that way." (To be continued)

CHARACTERISTICS OF EFFECTIVE TEAMS

There are two basic components to building effective teams: leaders, who provide vision and direction, and team members. A **team** may be described as a group of individuals who are united by a common mission with each member providing contributions that result in synergistic outcomes. Let's divide this statement into parts to illustrate the meaning of the description.

"A Group of Individuals"

A team is comprised of individuals. These people possess unique personalities, values, attitudes, and experiences. Some managers believe that teams are built by putting individuals together. This process does not create a team. What you get when you randomly put people together is a crowd. A crowd is not a team.

Because individuals vary in terms of backgrounds and beliefs, the potential exists for conflict among team members. Some managers believe that conflict is inappropriate. Actually, constructive conflict is healthy for team

Team—A group of individuals united by a common mission.

interaction and contributes to the effectiveness of team outcomes. However, the potential may exist for destructive forms of conflict. This type of conflict will serve to fragment team members, which is contrary to the purpose of teams.

Managers must respect and understand the individuality of team members. One method of conflict identification and resolution is to conduct team-building meetings that focus on individual personality awareness for the purpose of developing empathy and enhanced interpersonal relations. An experienced trainer should conduct these meetings and begin with an exercise to generate awareness of the different personality types possessed by individual group members. This type of work is reserved for highly trained facilitators with backgrounds in the behavioral sciences and management theory. It is sufficient for supervisors to remain aware that personality differences do exist among current and potential team members. With this in mind, the supervisor focuses on the mission for the group.

"United by a Common Mission"

Motivating missions have been identified as one key ingredient contributing to peak performance.[1] The team mission must be congruent with the values and beliefs of the team members (as discussed in transformational leadership in Chapter 3). This aspect is important for the selection of team members. In organizations, the mission for a department must flow from the mission for the organization. Likewise, the mission for the team members must flow from the mission for the department and the organization. When this happens, the entire organization becomes mission driven. Team members must have a personal stake in the mission. Therefore, the personal mission for each team member must be consistent with the mission for the team. Figure 9.1 provides sample mission statements for this purpose.[2]

"Contributing to Synergistic Outcomes"

This is the essence of the rationale for the development and maintenance of teams. Individuals are capable of producing individual outcomes. Groups of individuals are capable of producing group outcomes equal to the sum of the

---

The Organization Mission

To acquire and maintain guests and customers.
Grand Strategy: Anticipate and respond to guests' wants and desires.

The Mission for My Department or Work Area

To acquire and maintain guests and customers in my department.
Grand Strategy: Establish and maintain positive guest relationships.

My Personal Career Mission

To contribute to the mission for the department while achieving my career goals.
Grand Strategy: Enhance productivity in positions of progressive responsibility.

Figure 9–1.   Sample mission statements.

group's parts. Teams are capable of producing outcomes that exceed the sum of the parts. A team is comprised of individuals who are focused on one common mission. Each member brings unique knowledge and skills to the team. The combined knowledge and skills are formed into a contribution toward the entire outcome. Thus, the outcome is the result of a combined intensity of individual energy that exceeds the sum of its parts. So, in a *group* of four people, the outcome will be the sum of four individual efforts. Those same four individuals working as a *team* will produce an outcome equivalent to five or more individual efforts through teamwork. This is called **synergy.**

Synergy—The phenomenon by which the combined output is greater than the sum of its parts.

TEAM PLANNING

The objective of team management is to provide win-win-win processes.[3] The mission for the organization should be consistent with the mission for the department, which should be consistent with the personal missions of the team members. Everybody wins by contributing to a common cause.

Planning activities should include the win-win-win philosophy. The purpose of planning is to act in a proactive manner as opposed to a reactive manner. Items in the planning process should be prioritized by importance to the organization, the department, and the members. These tasks are both **critical** to the stakeholders and **crucial** in terms of required attention. Some managers spend most of their time focusing only on those items that are critical and not crucial. This is a short-term or reactive approach to prioritizing tasks. By focusing on matters that are crucial as well as critical, managers reduce the amount of time spent on reactive issues and focus on mission-driven issues. A critical issue is one that requires immediate action for some reason. A crucial issue is one that fulfills the mission of the company, department, and each team member. Some issues are critical but not crucial. For instance, the boss may require a last-minute report that will require 6 hours of preparation for some reason that has nothing to do with the mission of the business. This is critical because failure to produce the report could negatively impact the supervisor's job security. But since this has nothing to do with the mission, it is not crucial. At the same time, there is a group checking into the hotel today that will require personal attention and produce excellent revenues. This situation sounds to be both crucial and critical. What do we do? The experienced team leader will take care of the group first and produce the report later, even if this means she will have to apologize to the boss for turning that report in a

Critical tasks— Those activities that contribute to the mission for an organization.
Crucial tasks—Those tasks that must be performed immediately to avoid some sort of negative consequence.

HOSPITALITY TIPS & CLIPS *Show Your Appreciation*

As a supervisor, how will you express appreciation to your team members for their work, and to each individual as a person? Will team members show appreciation to each other often? It starts with management. Be sure to go out of your way to show your employees that you appreciate them!

Source: "Show Your Appreciation." *Hospitality News* (August 2002): p. 6. Courtesy of *Hospitality News.*

few hours late. The nonleader might hide in the office to produce the report and just hope all goes well with the group check-in. What type of message does this behavior send to the staff handling the group?

CRITICAL SUCCESS FACTORS

There are three types of critical success factors influencing successful outcomes of team planning. Virtually every factor influencing success may be listed within one of the categories. The categories are as follows:

- Material resources—These include equipment, supplies, physical plant, technology, and financial capital used to provide products or services.
- Human resources—These include human capital, staffing levels, knowledge, skills, and attitudes required for the production of products and services.
- Systems—These include organization, information, coordination, integration, and processing activities used to provide products and services.

CONFLICT

Managers sometimes assume that all forms of conflict are destructive. This is not true. Certain types of conflict may be constructive by contributing to the reshaping of ideas and concepts. Team leaders need to manage conflict to ensure that it is constructively contributing to decision-making activities. Below are suggestions for managing conflict:

- Recognize that differences are acceptable.

- Listen with understanding.
- Clarify reasons for conflict.
- Determine who will referee (third party).
- Set procedures/rules for resolution.
- Attend to the relationship of the disputants.
- Encourage communication between disputants.
- Close the conflict with communication.

The types of conflict fall within two categories. Personal conflicts are mostly created by ego, personality clashes, and differences of opinion, values, or priorities. Professional conflict results from disagreements concerning resource allocation and systems use/design.

FORMAL AND INFORMAL TEAM LEADERS

Formal leader—An individual appointed by an organization to a position of responsibility with the authority to delegate tasks.

Informal leader—An individual with the ability to influence others within an organization absent a position of authority to delegate tasks.

It was stated in the beginning of this section that teams require the guidance of appointed leaders. Appointed leaders are **formal leaders.** Individuals who are not appointed by the organization will surface as **informal leaders.** Informal leadership that is directed constructively for the welfare of the team and the organization should be encouraged by appointed leaders. There are two courses of action that may be taken when destructive informal leaders surface. One action would be to enlist the support of the informal leader for constructive purposes. A second course of action would be to eliminate the informal leader from the team. It is the job of the appointed leader to ensure the welfare of the team.

Appointed Team Leaders

The appointed, or formal, team leader is an individual who has evolved beyond the stage of managing people. This person continues to manage resources and systems. But when it comes to team members, the leader permits self-management. The leader of a team provides members with support, guidance, vision, and influence. The leader is usually an individual who has a vision of the future. He uses communication skills to articulate the team vision. He is usually passionate about the vision and communicates this passion in a manner that energizes team members to embrace the vision as their own. The leader also recognizes the importance of providing stewardship or support to members of the group. This involves adopting a client relationship with team members in which the leader accommodates the needs of those members. Finally, the leader influences team members to participate in "followership." The leader establishes a power base with the members of the team. He does this by exhibiting characteristics that create a willingness on the part of team members to follow him.

Sources of power include position, knowledge, expertise, and reference. Referent power is the strongest of these power bases. Truly effective leaders possess referent power of influence over others. Leaders with this power base are charismatic, confident, articulate, inspiring, supportive, and visionary. They possess and communicate a combination of characteristics that is so

---

HOSPITALITY TIPS & CLIPS *Trust: The Competitive Advantage*

It's been scientifically proven that managers who have the trust of their employees are at a competitive advantage in this day of the ebbing worker pool. A team of investigators asked more than 370 restaurant employees to rate how much they trust their general manager, and to rate the degree to which they had confidence in the manager's ability, integrity, and respect for employees.

They balanced those ratings against the operatives of the restaurants. Their findings:

Restaurants where employees trusted their managers achieved high levels of sales and profitability during the following quarter; and trusted managers were those with strong reputations for ability, integrity, and employee respect.

Source: "Trust: The Competitive Advantage." *Hospitality News* (April 2002): p. 22. Courtesy of *Food Industry News.*

---

appealing that they create a strong sense of personal trust and loyalty among the members of the team. This referent power base is sometimes referred to as the "personal power" of the leader.

EMPLOYEE TURNOVER

Employee turnover— The number of workers who separate from positions in an organization and require replacement.

New workers require a period of time for the introduction to team membership. They should be exposed to systematic activities for assimilation into the team or work unit. Failure to adequately assimilate new workers contributes to premature **employee turnover.** Highly cohesive teams sometimes present difficulties associated with new worker assimilation. Employment selection, orientation, training, and mentoring by members of the team are strategies that enhance the likelihood of new worker assimilation.

THE BUBBLE THEORY OF MANAGING INTERPERSONAL RELATIONS

One researcher provides the "nucleus theory" of managing interpersonal relations with lateral members of the organizational structure.[4] We call this the Bubble Theory of managing interpersonal relations.

Imagine yourself and your department as being contained within a bubble. Along the edge of the bubble there are other bubbles, which represent those departments or individuals you rely upon to effectively accomplish tasks. A sample Bubble Management Chart is presented in Figure 9.2.

Bubble Management in Practice

The experienced department manager will view the organizational positioning of the department in a way that is similar to this chart. The manager realizes that the success of the department team depends on linkages with teams

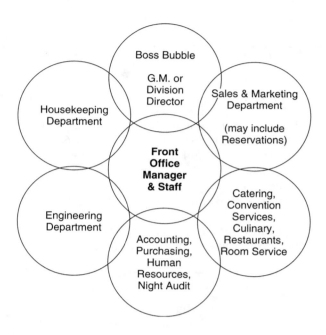

Figure 9–2.

in the surrounding bubbles. The manager also recognizes the importance of maintaining working relationships with representatives from these teams. The Boss Bubble includes the senior administrative assistants. While these people have no formal authority over the department manager, they are important links to the president, general manager, and executive committee members. Administrative assistants are sometimes referred to as "gatekeepers." They guard access to the executive offices and influence the executives' opinions concerning various department managers. The savvy department manager is cognizant of the importance of secretarial personnel due to their professional relationships with the bosses.

While the Boss Bubble may be the most intruding force on the department, it does not require as high a level of maintenance as some of the other bubbles. For instance, the crucial bubbles for the hotel front office manager would include the housekeeping, engineering, and sales functions. These areas require closer linkages than some of the other areas. Thus, these are areas in which more effort is expended to establish and maintain interdepartmental relations.

Organizational Bank Accounts

Every individual who represents a department in a bubble possesses an organizational bank account with each department on the bubble. The organizational bank account is similar to a financial bank account in that people make deposits and withdrawals. Like a financial bank account, the objective of the organizational bank account is to avoid becoming overdrawn. Ideally, one would want the deposits in the organizational bank account to exceed withdrawals, just like a financial bank account with a positive balance.

Organizational Currency

While the currency in a financial bank account is money, organizational currency is in the form of "favors" and cooperation with other department managers. A front office manager who has done many favors for members of departments linked to the front office bubble will build up a positive balance in the organizational bank account with that department. Also, the other department managers learn that they can count on the front office manager to help out in times of need. This is known as the "organizational credit rating." A positive bank balance and a high credit rating among comanagers means the front office manager will receive cooperation from other departments on a regular basis.

While a high interdepartmental credit rating warrants high levels of cooperation and support from members from other departments, managers with low credit ratings find themselves in a position in which other departments will not be willing to lend support to them or their departments. In the case of the front office manager, a high credit rating with the housekeeping department (based on a high account balance) will result in fast inventory turns, concise information, cooperation in preparing rooms for check-in, and occasional special favors. If the front office manager maintains a poor rating with the sales department (low bank account balance) it is likely that group rooming information will be slower and less accurate, rooming blocks will be incomplete, guarantees will not be communicated, and contracts or billing information may be unavailable.

A poor credit rating with a single department may cause a ripple effect to other departments on the bubble. For instance, the poor credit rating with the sales department will slow down the flow of group check-in information, which is passed on to other operating departments. Let's say that a group is scheduled to receive amenity fruit baskets, which are prepared by members

of the culinary department. The room service department may be responsible for delivering the fruit baskets to the guest rooms. If the sales department releases the group rooming information at the last minute, the amenity orders go to the culinary department at the last minute, and the room service staff will have to deliver the baskets at the last moment. In this case, a poor relationship between front office and sales has created a hardship for the culinary and room service departments. Who gets the blame? The front office manager and staff. The front office manager then blames the sales manager, which worsens the front office manager's credit rating with the sales department.

Some managers have the misconception that their sole purpose is to make the boss happy. In the pursuit of this quest, they alienate workers and comanagers. They make themselves look good at the expense of their comanagers. They do this by shifting blame to other departments and taking all the credit for performance success. For a short period of time, these managers establish very "fat" bank accounts with their bosses, at the expense of their comanagers. Eventually, the boss is faced with the dilemma of supporting the manager who is alienating other departments. An inexperienced boss may decide to declare bankruptcy in all other bank accounts by seeking to replace the other department managers. On the other hand, an experienced boss will recognize that one manager is seeking accolades at the expense of the other managers.

There are five performance criteria. They are the same criteria used among managers and workers. They include: expectations, procedures, resources, accountability, and consequences. A manager must meet the expectations and procedures of comanagers. The manager must share resources with them. The manager must be accountable for interactions among comanagers. Finally, the manager will receive the consequences of the actions, not from a boss, but from other managers. Therefore, organizational bank deposits involve interacting with other managers in ways that meet expectations and procedures, while sharing resources and levels of accountability. Conversely, failing to meet expectations, refusal to comply with procedures, hoarding of resources, and pointing blame will result in bank account withdrawals. A bank deposit has the consequence of collaboration. Too many bank withdrawals have the consequence of lack of cooperation. Plenty of withdrawals with no deposits results in overdrawn accounts with departments on the bubble. A number of overdrawn accounts will result in departmental bankruptcy. When the department becomes organizationally bankrupt, it's "out of business" as far as support from lateral departments. Eventually, the bosses in the organization will realize the need to change the management of the department. If the entire organization becomes bankrupt, the shareholders will be likely to make the management change.

SUMMARY

The purpose of a team is to attain synergistic outcomes. There are two basic components to a team: the leaders and members. Most teams are self-directed, and leadership may vary from a single appointed leader to a varying degree of adoption of leadership roles by team members. The difference between a team and a group or crowd is the focus of the members. A team consists of membership that is focused on individual and group contribution to a single set of outcomes, which are driven by the mission of the team. Effective teams consist of members who are dedicated to a team mission, which is congruent with the personal missions of the team players. The human phenomenon of conflict is likely to occur among members of a team. Conflict must be managed to ensure that it remains constructive to the overall outcomes desired by the team.

... *In the Real World* (Continued)

The guys buy you another drink, so you continue with the story. "It wasn't always that way," you say. "I started there as a busser when I was in school. Back then it was like any other restaurant. But then Louis came along. We called him 'Coach.' It started as a joke and then it just stuck. He has worked every job there is in this business and has even owned his own restaurant. The owners really wanted him to work for the company and finally convinced him to come on board as the GM of our store.

"Rumor has it that when Louis first started, he asked the owners for a realistic expectation of the store's financial performance in terms of revenues and profits. He then cut a deal with them that if we surpassed their goals, they would give him a portion of the incremental earnings to distribute at his own discretion. They agreed. His final stipulation with the owners was that he would have complete freedom to be creative in the management of the store with no interference from corporate personnel. They agreed.

"With this deal, Louis was ready to make his debut at our restaurant. He watched us work for a few days, and then he started talking with us one on one. He spent most of his time with the management team. Most of those guys really hated him, and some of them left. He replaced the open positions with individuals he had worked with in the past. He then set up all the basics for the store. You know, mission, objectives, strategies, policies, standards, procedures, and stuff like that. Then he put together this great training program for every job in the restaurant. He made it mandatory for everyone to go through the training sessions, while the rest of his management team started holding everyone strictly accountable for meeting or exceeding the standards. Well, now *most* of the staff hated him and they started to leave in droves. It was like Louis had this all planned; as soon as someone left, he would have a replacement who had worked with him in the past. You get the picture, he set up the basics back then."

You continue, "It took Louis about a year to get us to where we are now. Everyone is an 'owner,' so to speak, because every fiscal quarter that incremental money I told you about gets distributed to us. So, you can imagine the level of peer pressure levied against anyone who wastes money, doesn't sell, or upsets our guests. Louis has simply created the best working team I have ever had the pleasure to be a part of."

QUESTIONS FOR DISCUSSION

1. There are those who contend that the word "team" is so overused that it has lost its true meaning. Do you think this is true? If you do, how did this happen?

2. Which leadership style do you think is appropriate for the development of teams? Trait, transactional, or transformational? Why?

3. Is it absolutely necessary to build teams all the time? Are there times when functional groups are good enough? Why or why not?

MINI-CASE

You are a supervisor for a small work unit consisting of five workers. The previous two supervisors were fired for poor performance. Needless to say, the workers are doubtful about whether you will be any more successful than your predecessors. It is interesting that the work group has sort of bonded as a result of poor leadership and is pretty self-sufficient when it comes to doing the job. You know that the first thing you must do is to earn their respect. Once this is done, you will want to build a team.

Question:

How will you earn their respect and then build a team?

Hint:

Setting a good example and demonstrating stewardship could help with both objectives.

 KEY TERMS

Critical task	Employee	Formal leader	Synergy
Crucial task	turnover	Informal leader	

CHAPTER QUIZ

1.	All groups are not teams.	T	F
2.	Teams produce synergistic outcomes.	T	F
3.	Team building does not require any special skills.	T	F
4.	Conflict is always a bad thing in teams.	T	F
5.	Formal leaders are those appointed by the organization.	T	F
6.	Critical success factors include resources, systems, and outcomes.	T	F
7.	Accountability is included in performance criteria.	T	F
8.	The Bubble Theory says that supervisors need not worry about peers.	T	F
9.	Organizational currency takes the form of favors for other supervisors.	T	F
10.	Supervisors must cooperate with other managers to be successful.	T	F

ENDNOTES

1. Don Delves, "Trend or Foe?" *Strategic Finance* 84, no. 6 (December 2002): 36.
2. Charles R. Duke, "Learning Outcomes: Comparing Student Perceptions of Skill Level and Importance," *Journal of Marketing Education* 24, no. 3 (December 2002): 203.
3. Carla Joinson, "No Returns," *HRMagazine* 47, no. 11 (November 2002): 70.
4. Lillian T. Eby, "Further Investigation of Protégés' Negative Mentoring Experiences: Patterns and Outcomes," *Group & Organization Management* 27, no. 4 (December 2002): 456.

CHAPTER TEN
Measuring Performance

OBJECTIVES

At the end of this chapter, readers will be able to:

1. Understand the role of employee appraisal as one part of a holistic performance management system.
2. Identify performance standards as the benchmark for measuring performance.
3. Recognize common formal appraisal formats.
4. Understand the role of the supervisor as providing daily informal appraisals.

Performance management system—A system of expectations, training, and assessment of performance for workers in an organization.

This chapter presents a systems approach to performance management. The preceding chapters in this book have identified all the supervision subsystems that result in the **performance management system.** A performance management system provides identification, encouragement, and evaluation of actual performance, as it relates to established performance standards. The purpose of performance measurement is to provide feedback to employees about their performance and to take actions to facilitate improvement, as well as provide recognition of successful performance levels by giving rewards. Actually, this is not a stand-alone process, as some managers would have us believe. Instead, it is a multidisciplinary approach to people management that requires daily observation and communication through coaching, mentoring, and disciplinary warnings on the part of the supervisor. The effectiveness of these practices is related to the levels of awareness on the part of the supervisor concerning the service perspective, leadership practice, worker motivation, and work life development.

PERFORMANCE STANDARDS

The performance management process starts with performance standards, which are simply behavioral goals. Then, job criteria (referred to as job lists) are established, which prioritize the importance of each job function by listing the procedures to meet each standard. The worker exceeds, meets, or does not meet each category of performance. Since some aspects of performance are more important than others, we attach mathematical weights (10 percent, 50 percent, etc.) to each performance category. Next, we multiply the weights (percentages) times each category. The averaged total will provide an indication of the overall performance levels. For instance, if the worker exceeds standards for a criterion that is 60 percent of the job and meets the rest, that worker is above the standards (or an excellent performer, as most managers like to say). The process just described is called a performance appraisal.

Effectiveness—Generating outputs that meet standards for quality and quantity.

Efficiency—Procuring and using resources in a way that minimizes the cost of inputs.

What is the basis of performance standards? You learned this already: it is the productivity model, which measures **effectiveness** and **efficiency.** Customer relationship issues such as service levels and product quality/quantity are measures of effectiveness. Reducing resource expenses is an efficiency measurement. For example, a server in a full-service restaurant provides excellent guest service in a station consisting of 12 covers (seats). That server is being effective. Another server provides the same level of service in a station with 20 covers. That server is both effective and efficient because she is meeting the quality standards for eight more guests than the other server. If every server had this ability, there would be fewer servers required to staff the restaurant, which will result in lower payroll costs without compromising service quality. If the supervisor were to staff the restaurant in stations of 20 covers with the servers providing mediocre service, the restaurant would be efficient, but not effective. Thus the supervisor would be meeting only part of his performance responsibility.

PERFORMANCE APPRAISAL METHODS

There are two types of performance appraisals. One is done daily and is mostly verbal. This is an informal appraisal. The formal appraisal is written (usually on a performance appraisal form) and occurs on a periodic basis (usually annually). Who appraises whom? Well, supervisors always appraise their workers, but workers could appraise their supervisors as well; this is called the *180-degree model*. In some cases, subordinates, supervisors, and peers participate in the appraisal process. This is the *360-degree model*. Peer ratings are becoming popular with the push toward self-managed teams. Almost all ratings are multisource as they usually include one extra step up in the chain of command. Self-evaluations are good introspection tools. However, most people lack the level of self-awareness to do this function effectively. If you use customer feedback, plus all the other ratings mentioned here, you are truly doing a multisource rating.

There are various formal appraisal methods. The most popular is the category rating method, which includes graphic rating scales (1–5) and checklist methods (check off the statement that applies). Comparative methods rate employees against each other. Ranking methods rank them from best to worst. Forced distribution puts most in the middle and a few at each end (like the bell curve for grading). Narrative methods involve writing reports based on performance observations. Figure 10.1 provides an example of a formal performance appraisal form used for most service positions.

A powerful tool is the critical incident method that combines informal with formal reviews. You as a manager take notes on your observations of important (critical) activities (incidents) for each employee (this was discussed in Chapter 8). You take five minutes daily to place the notes in a file marked for each worker. At the end of the year, voila, you have a year's worth of notes on each worker's performance (a powerful tool).

Behavioral approaches focus on specific job behaviors that are predefined by some document. Management by objectives (MBO) is both a goal-setting activity and a performance appraisal method. It involves top/down, bottom/up goals to be set for every level of the organization based on the mission. Supervisors then review the accomplishment of objectives at some later date. In actual practice, the performance appraisal system may be a hybrid of many methods that have been mentioned in this chapter.

There are factors known collectively as *rater error* that may invalidate the performance appraisal. *Recency effect* occurs when you don't use the critical incident method and can remember only the last few weeks of performance for each worker. *Central tendency error* is when you try to make everyone average. *Rater bias* occurs when personal issues cloud the objective criteria of the review. *Halo effect* is rating all categories on one attribute. *Contrast error* occurs when comparisons are made to other workers instead of to objective criteria.

The most important part of a formal review is the interview. It should be done in private, be a two-way dialog, and only occur after the person being reviewed has had sufficient time to read the completed appraisal document. The worst thing for a supervisor to do is to avoid issues that may be less than positive. People have a tendency to do this because we don't like to deliver bad news. This practice is dishonest on the part of the supervisor and will ultimately result in negative consequences for both parties. However, in the process of delivering negative information, supervisors are cautioned to always be kind and compassionate with their interactive style.

As far as legal aspects of performance appraisals, supervisors should be sure the methods used are valid, reliable, fair, uniform, and consistent. This rule is true for any supervisory practice.

SUMMARY

What makes a performance management system a "system"? The mission for the organization, which is used to develop objective performance standards, drives a performance management system. The standards are broken down into policies and procedures for each task that is driven by these standards. Managers and supervisors symbolize the service perspective in their daily

Name: _____ Due Date: _____

Department: _____ Job Title: _____

Date of Last Review: _____ Start Date in Position: _____

Next Scheduled Review: _____ Type of Review: _____

Factors	Does Not Meet (3)	Meets (2)	Exceeds (1)
1. Scheduled shifts attended			
2. Timely attendance			
3. Quality of work			
4. Quantity of work			
5. Timely completion of work			
6. Teamwork and cooperation			
7. Sanitation and maintenance			
8. Grooming standards			
9. Safety and accidents			
10. Contribution to Guest Service Index			
Total Points			

Strengths:

Areas for Improvement:

Reviewer's Comments:

Reviewee's Comments:

Reviewer Signature _____ Date _____

Reviewee Signature _____ Date _____

Figure 10–1.

interactions. They are aware of human motivational factors and take a personal interest in the work life development of the staff members. They engage in sound leadership practices, through which they employ effective communication skills used to coach, recognize, evaluate, counsel, and use progressive discipline with the staff members in appropriate situations. Managers and supervisors employ the critical incident method to account for all important

HOSPITALITY TIPS & CLIPS *Determining Who Should Get a Raise*

Every staff member would like a raise in pay. But deciding how much additional compensation to give an employee is often confusing. Try this method from the late George Odiorne, who has been called America's premier expert regarding management by objectives.

- If an employee is below par in performing routine responsibilities, she should not be kept in that position or should be given training and time to improve. No raise is warranted.
- If the person is performing routine duties but doing nothing more, he is fulfilling the job description and is entitled to the same job (at the same pay) for another year.
- Raises and bonuses should go to the individual who contributes to the progress of the business and does not simply fulfill routine duties. Staff members who actively participate in solving problems by offering helpful ideas are worth more to your company and should be awarded a raise or additional compensation.

Source: "Determining Who Should Get a Raise." *Hospitality News* (August 2002): p. 23. Courtesy of *Hospitality News*.

aspects of performance. Finally, they provide constructive feedback to the workers through performance appraisal methods, which are used to redirect behaviors below the standards and to develop the careers of workers who meet or exceed the standards. Thus we began the system with the first chapter of the book and complete the system with this conclusive chapter on supervision in the service industry.

. . . *In the Real World (Continued)*

Before you have had a chance to talk with the banquet manager about your performance appraisal, you receive a call from the catering director (the banquet manager's supervisor) to meet with her and the banquet manager in her office at an appointed time.

You arrive for the meeting and take a seat. Joe, the banquet manager, begins to speak to you as Jane, the catering director, observes. Joe says, "Jane informed me that performance appraisals are more involved here than they were at my last hotel. So I did my homework and revised your appraisal. I would like to share my findings with you."

Joe continues, "First, I looked at your personnel file and found many very complimentary guest comments. The guests really love your service, which is a great contribution to the department. Also, I reviewed your former appraisals and noticed you have consistently been rated as an excellent employee. I compared my observations of your performance to the standards of service for the banquet department and must admit, you exceed every one of them. So, I would like you to take some time to review my ratings and comments and feel free to discuss anything you like about your position here," Joe concludes.

As you review the form, you think to yourself, "I thought other hotels were as good as this one. I think I'll stay here for awhile."

QUESTIONS FOR DISCUSSION

1. Some people believe that managers just fill out performance appraisal forms without giving them much thought. Do you think this is true? How would you feel if someone did that to you?

2. A manager runs a department in which everyone is above average. He leaves and a new manager takes over. When the new manager does appraisals, she rates everyone as average. How can this be if there has been no change in performance?

3. You sit down with the manager for your performance appraisal interview. The manager starts citing dates and times of specific behaviors performed by you over the past year. Do you think that manager has a photographic memory, or is he using some other technique? Would you use such a technique? Why or why not?

MINI-CASE

You are hired as the manager for a department that is in need of improvement. You assess the situation by walking around and conducting individual discussions with each employee. You find that there is a general feeling of apathy among all the staff members. Usually you can find some workers whom you can turn around, but you are beginning to believe that this is not the case with anyone on this crew. You are starting to come to the conclusion that you may have to "clean house" in this department. You mentally consider doing a mass hiring session to replace every position.

You go down to the human resources office and review the files of your crew members. To your surprise, you find that they have all been rated at levels of above average to excellent over the past 3 years!

Question:

Now what do you do?

Hint:

You must be fair, uniform, and consistent in your management practices.

KEY TERMS

Effectiveness   Efficiency   Performance
                                       management
                                       system

CHAPTER QUIZ

1.	A performance management system provides effective supervision.	T	F
2.	An appraisal compares actual performance to standards.	T	F
3.	A formal appraisal is written on a periodic basis.	T	F
4.	Supervisors conduct informal appraisals every day.	T	F
5.	A 360-degree appraisal includes peers and subordinates.	T	F
6.	MBO is a participative management and appraisal tool.	T	F
7.	Feedback is given to workers during the appraisal interview.	T	F
8.	A performance management system should be driven by the mission.	T	F
9.	Efficiency is maximizing use of resources.	T	F
10.	Effectiveness is maximizing quality and quantity of outputs.	T	F

CHAPTER ELEVEN

Getting a Job or Promotion

OBJECTIVES

At the end of this chapter, readers will be able to:

1. Understand the basics of conducting a job search.
2. Build a convincing resume.
3. Understand how to network for position opportunities.
4. Understand the basics of interviewing skills.

In the Real World. . .

You are ready to graduate from school at the end of this semester. During your school years you worked front- and back-line positions at a country club, freestanding restaurant, hotel, and convention center. You received excellent evaluations in all of your jobs. You have the names and contact information for all of your former bosses. Each of them would love for you to join them as a full-time supervisor after you graduate.

Unfortunately, this situation isn't true for most of your friends. They are hoping to get management jobs when they graduate, but haven't had much experience and don't really even know where to start. (To be continued)

Now that you have learned the ins and outs of supervision, you may want to attain a position as a supervisor or manager. Some individuals choose to study full-time and are starting their job search from scratch. Others are currently employed and are seeking an advanced position. Regardless of your situation, you are about to embark on an endeavor that will test your endurance, self-esteem, creativity, and tenacity. Few people actually enjoy the process of searching for a position; yet all of us find ourselves faced with this task from time to time. Therefore, you are not alone!

This chapter is designed to help you with job search basics. Topics include prospecting, written communications, interviewing, and other issues presented from the viewpoint of individuals who make hiring decisions for organizations. As is the case with the preceding chapters in this book, the information is presented in a straightforward manner for you to use in the job search process. This chapter contains examples to help you plan and implement your search.

WHAT DO I WANT TO DO?

For most of us, deciding on the type of job that will provide satisfaction can be a difficult process. Usually, people ask themselves, "What do I want to do for a living?" This seems like a simple question to answer. However, many of us have pondered this simple question for years before reaching a suitable decision. Some people change careers at points in their lives when they realize that they no longer enjoy their present field of work. So, if you are having trouble finding a conclusive answer to the question of what type of work will be most satisfying to you, you are like many of us.

Some people find success using a process of elimination in the search for the ideal job. That is, they consider those things they *don't* want to do for a living. Unfortunately, this approach can be time consuming. Professional instruments are available to identify preferred career interests. One example is the Strong-Campbell Interest Inventory. Other scientific tests predict job preferences based on personality indicators. Examples include the Myers-Briggs Type Indicator and the Kersey-Bates Temperament Sorter.

Most instruments identify preferences for performing certain types of activities. The characteristics of certain jobs may then be compared to those preferred activities. For instance, if it is determined that an individual likes to work alone, enjoys investigative activities, prefers to use logic, and likes working with numbers, she may enjoy working as an accountant or financial analyst. On the other hand, a person who is outgoing, likes working with people, needs freedom to move about, and enjoys helping others may prefer a front-line position in hospitality or other service-oriented positions.

The bottom line is—you and only you can decide the type of work that will bring you personal satisfaction. Do you remember the mountain climber from a previous chapter? Let's say that you are the climber. You stand at the base of a large mountain. You begin your climb. As you progress along the way, you struggle more and more to navigate the steep terrain. With your last ounce of energy, you pull yourself to the top of the mountain. You stand on the summit and look around—only to find you have climbed the wrong mountain! This metaphor describes what can happen if we pursue goals that are not really the ones we want to achieve. Sometimes we find ourselves pursuing other people's goals. We should be sure to pursue those things that really have value to us, regardless of what others may think.

HOSPITALITY TIPS & CLIPS   *The Perfect Match: Finding a Career That Fits You!*

With so many job opportunities out there, how does a student find a career that fits her interests and abilities? Here are a few things you should try:

Find a part-time job. Find a company that you are interested in and see if you can get an inside look at their operation. Granted, you may be filing, or, in the case of a restaurant, busing tables, but be observant and watch how the professionals spend their day.

Volunteer. If a company you are interested in doesn't have a part-time job opportunity, then volunteer. Let the employer know you are contemplating this type of work as a future career. Almost every occupation accepts volunteers for some part of their operation. Community bulletin boards and local newspapers are good places to look for volunteer opportunities.

Job shadow. In a job shadow situation, you will team up with a person doing a particular job for a day or two. Ask many questions and get a first-hand look at the position. Call the employer of a company you are interested in and ask if there are job shadow opportunities available.

Intern. Once you've begun your education, start asking your teachers about internship opportunities. Some are paid positions while others are unpaid, but an internship offers you a chance to try out a job that interests you.

Find a mentor. Discover a person who is doing a job that you see yourself eventually doing. Call and ask if the person would consider being your mentor as you start your career. Inquire about his likes and dislikes of the position. Most adults love to help students who are eager and interested in what they are doing. To begin a mentoring relationship, you might want to see if the potential mentor would let you drop by for a half-hour interview. Arrive prepared with questions about the person's job.

Source: "The Perfect Match: Finding a Career That Fits You!" *Hospitality News* 1, no. 1 (Fall 2001): p. 4. Courtesy of *Hospitality News.*

HOW TO START A JOB SEARCH

It would be appropriate to adopt a strategic approach to searching for a position. Once you have reached a conclusion (or at least have a few ideas) about what it is you want to do, you have established your job search mission. Your mission is the general purpose of your career decision and is stated very broadly. A few examples of career mission statements are:

- "A rewarding career in hotel or cruise industry operations"
- "To work in the field of human resources management for a service-based organization"
- "A progressive sales career that will provide opportunities for unlimited personal income"

It is important to avoid confusing the career mission statement with the job search objective. The mission represents your career aspirations or purpose. The immediate objective relates to the goals of the current job search.

The next step in the strategic job search process is to conduct research. For those who are graduating from college, this is not the same as academic research. This type of research consists of conducting a practical investigation of opportunities, organizations, and types of positions. One way to do this is to talk with as many practitioners as you can in your chosen field. Printed and electronic information may be available in the form of websites, newsletters, trade magazines, professional employment organizations, and other sources. Counseling may be provided to job seekers through firms that specialize in job placement for specific industries or job functions. Other sources of information may include vocational counselors, executive search firms, and recruiters.

After the research is completed, identify the specific job to be targeted through your search. This is your job search objective. Examples of job search objectives are:

- "To obtain an entry-level supervisory position in food and beverage management with a medium to large hotel or resort"
- "To obtain a sales and marketing position with a progressive organization providing opportunities for growth based on performance"

Once you have determined your job search objective, everything you do is based on this goal. Please notice two things. First, the job search objective statement is more specific than your career mission statement. Second, your objective is passive, which means it is a target that you will reach by performing action steps aimed toward the attainment of this goal.

JOB SEARCH STRATEGIES

Once you have established your job search objective, the next step is to develop strategies (action steps) to accomplish the objective. It is recommended that job searchers plan their work and work their plan. This will maximize your time investment and minimize redundancy of activities. The EPIC

Establish a resume and reference list.
Prospect activities to make contact with those individuals who may
   provide opportunities for interviews.
Interview in a manner that will result in further consideration for the job.
Correspond, aimed at further consideration for the job.

Figure 11–1.   EPIC model.

model presented in Figure 11.1 provides headings for your job search strategic activities.

Notice that these strategies focus on specific activities. Each activity takes the job searcher one step further in the recruitment and selection process. Also, notice that these action steps do not end with receiving an offer of employment. That is because getting the job is the overall objective of the search. Before the overall objective is attained, each job search goal for each job search strategy must be attained in sequence. Examples of goals for a job search that result in the achievement of the overall objective are as follows:

- Contact recruiters for targeted companies.
- Present a resume that will entice them to grant you an interview.
- Convince the interviewer to continue the selection process with you as a candidate.
- Convince the decision maker that you are the most qualified applicant for the position.

Now that we have a job search mission, objectives, and strategies, we are ready to establish a plan outline for finding a position as a supervisor. A sample plan is listed below:

I. Establish a resume and reference list.
    a. Write a resume and cover letter.
    b. Compile a reference list.
    c. Edit the resume, cover letter, and reference list.
    d. Provide a sufficient supply for distribution.

II. Prospect for interviews.
    a. Network.
    b. Utilize an executive search and other recruiting sources.
    c. Pursue employment leads (advertising, hearsay, etc.).
    d. Send or present resumes and cover letters to qualified leads.
    e. Follow up as appropriate.

III. Interview.
    a. Obtain a preliminary interview (get the next interview).
    b. Qualify for an advanced interview (compete to be the best qualified for the job).
    c. Complete other pre-employment qualifying activities.

IV. Correspond to convince prospective employers to start and continue the selection process.
 a. Prospect recruiters.
 b. Prepare a resume that gets you the preliminary interview.
 c. Convince the recruiter to consider you further.
 d. Convince the advanced interviewers that you are the most qualified applicant.

At this point the job searcher is ready to implement the job search plan.

HOW TO IMPLEMENT THE PLAN

The job search plan is simply an outline of the mission, objectives, and activities to be used in finding a supervisory position. There are skills required to effectively complete a job search. The two basic skills are effective writing skills and effective interviewing skills.

There are four major elements in conducting a successful job search. The first element is the resume and other written documents. The second is the ability to contact individuals who are involved in hiring for the position you want. Third is your professional image. The fourth element is the ability to interview effectively. Each of these elements is addressed in the following sections.

Resumes and Correspondence

Regardless of who is reading your resume, it is important to remember that the person is charged with reading numerous documents and most likely will not be willing to invest the time to carefully read your documents. Also, it is important to note that the reader is looking for a reason to put your resume in the "Thanks, but no thanks" file. The reader is performing a selection process called "screening." Screening is designed to limit the number of resumes that make it to the second phase of the selection process. It usually is not feasible to grant every interested party an interview. Therefore, individuals (usually human resources practitioners) screen written documents for the purpose of selecting individuals who clearly stand out from the others in terms of fit for the requirements of the position. They will recommend a small number of applicants for preliminary interviews. The remaining resumes are placed in a "dead" file. In some cases a form letter is sent to thank senders for their interest and to notify them that the resume will be "kept on file." The majority of firms do not even provide the courtesy of a response to your job inquiry if they do not intend to invite you for an interview. This doesn't mean the organization is cold and uncaring; often, there are too few staff members and too little use of technology to respond to all inquiries.

According to one source, the average resume receives about 5 seconds of attention.[1] During that time the reader may only give a cursory glance at the resume if she is distracted by other activities. For instance, a resume that lands on the desk of a human resources practitioner indicates that the writer is seeking a position as an administrative assistant. If that company is not actively seeking an administrative assistant, the resume is likely to be filed without being read. This is unfortunate, since there may be similar positions that would be suitable to the applicant's knowledge, skills, and abilities. While this information may sound a bit depressing, it is the way things really do work in corporations. Many people write resumes with the expectation that the recipient will review them with interest and enthusiasm. Unfortunately, due to volume and time constraints, this is not the case with most companies.

There are numerous publications that provide resume writing assistance. There are also many theories on how to construct the best resume. In actuality, there is no one best format. However, there are a few rules of thumb that would apply to most resumes. First and foremost, remember your audience when constructing a resume. The reader will, at best, skim down the center of the first page of your resume. A resume should usually be no more than two pages in length. For less experienced individuals (5 years or less), one page is usually sufficient. The big advantage to a one-page resume is that there is no second page that can be detached and lost.

A resume should have plenty of white space on each page. That is to say, the words should be formatted in a manner that leaves plenty of unused space on each page. This provides for easy reading. Also, 12-point, plain font should be used for the text of the resume. While word-processing software provides the ability to easily use many different font types, this may be distracting to the reader. A rule of thumb is that no more than two font types should be used. The use of bold lettering for headings, qualifications, positions, and employers is appropriate, as it creates stand-out text for easy spotting of important information.

Margins should be 1 inch or more on each side of the page. Top and bottom margins may be minimal. The resume should be printed on quality stock bonded paper. Even photocopies can be placed on bonded paper. Avoid the use of parchment or types of stock that hamper easy reading of the resume. Contrast is important; black print on white paper is recommended. If you are using a printer, be sure it provides quality lettering and that the print is sufficiently dark. It is amazing that many people send resumes with faded print.

The paper should be clean and wrinkle-free. Corners of the pages should not be tattered. Spelling and grammar should be correct. While these seem like commonsense rules of thumb, the frequency with which people overlook these details is quite high. Also, it is important to remember that you won't be there to explain any errors. Therefore, the paper is an impression of you. Remember, the person who is reviewing the resume is looking for an excuse to stop reading and place the resume in the "dead" file.

As a general rule, there are five sections of a resume. However, remember what we said before: There is no one correct format. You may choose to include those sections that you feel fit your circumstances. The five general sections are the heading, the job objective, the listing of accomplishments or qualifications, the career summary, and the credentials.

The Heading   The heading should contain contact information for the applicant: name, address, phone number, and email address. Human resources professionals report large numbers of resumes received without telephone numbers or email addresses listed in the heading section. Without this information, how is the reader supposed to contact the applicant for an interview? You can imagine just how much effort would be expended to track this type of applicant down. One might ask, "If I am currently employed, should I include my work number?" The answer to this question depends on the level of privacy you have at work and the confidentiality of your search, not to mention your current employer's policy on the use of company telephones. The heading may be centered or placed near the left or right margin at the top of each page. You may ask, "Why should I include a full heading on each page?" The pages of your resume may become detached. In the event of a lost page, the heading will provide an easy match to the other page.

The Job Objective   The job objective appears below the heading of the resume. Be sure to double-space your lines. The job or position should be specific and plainly worded. It should not exceed four lines of type (two to three are ideal). The objective may be prefaced with the word "**OBJECTIVE:**" in bold print, followed by your objective statement. You may choose to use underlining as opposed to bold print. However, a rule of thumb is that underlining and bold print should not be used together with the same words.

The Listing of Accomplishments or Qualifications   A listing of skills, accomplishments, or qualifications that are relevant to the position may be provided. This section would appear below the objective section (double spaced). You may choose to use bullets for each item listed. This provides a nice touch and enhances the readability of the resume. You should list no more than five or six items in this section. Each item in the list should be no more than one to two lines in length. Figure 11.2 displays an example of this section.

Summary of Qualifications

- Proven ability to supervise operations and enhance productivity.
- Demonstrated ability to assist with management interventions aimed at improving departmental performance.
- Strong leadership, motivation, and communication skills.

Figure 11–2.   Sample listing of qualifications.

Notice that the use of bullets eliminates the need to double-space between items listed.

The Career Summary   The career summary is usually the longest portion of the resume. Many resume writers choose to provide a chronological listing of their job history. Human resources practitioners usually prefer this format. Another style is to use a functional listing. This may be appropriate for individuals who are demonstrating professional skills and accomplishments over many years. This style lessens or eliminates the use of dates. Chronological career summaries are most common and are expected by readers in most companies.

With the chronological format, as a general rule, the description of the current or most recent position will use more space than other positions that are listed. Progressively less space is afforded to each position as the writer works back in time. Another rule of thumb is to include no more than 10 years of experience in the summary. Again, this is not carved in stone. You may want the prospective employer to know that you were a senior accountant 11 years ago. Also, many individuals have not accumulated 10 years of experience. In these cases, the resume writer may afford more space to describing each position held, if appropriate.

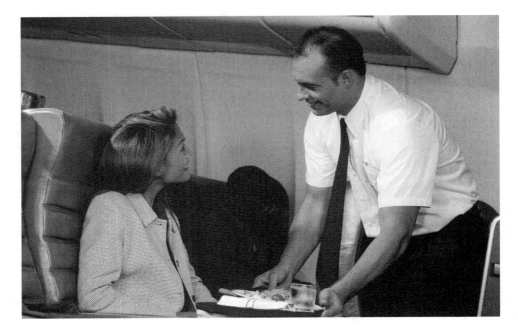

A heading should appear for each position, starting with the most recent position held. The headings may be in bold print. Dates for each position may appear to the left of the heading. Two spaces below the heading, a brief description of the organization and duties, as well as accomplishments of the position may appear in paragraph form. Short phrases or even incomplete sentences are appropriate for each description. An example of a position appearing in a career summary is provided in Figure 11.3.

Notice the short phrases in the description. Also, the first three accomplishments occurred in the past. Therefore, they are described in past tense terms. The last accomplishment is ongoing. Thus, it is listed in the present tense. The position before the current one would use less description space, the one before that even less, and so on. Ultimately, the earliest position may simply use dates of employment and the position title. The example used the month and year format, while some writers use just the years of employment. The method to use depends on the preference of the resume writer. Sometimes writers list years of employment to cover gaps, so this may raise a red flag in the mind of the reader.

The Credentials   While education and credentials are important for many reasons, they may not be the primary considerations for determining qualifications for certain jobs. Since other qualifications usually weigh more heavily, the credentials section usually appears last on the resume. However, if, for instance, you are a recent college graduate with little full-time experience, you may choose to list your academic credentials and certifications first on the resume under the qualifications summary. Even if you do not have much full-time experience, you still have skills and abilities learned in school or on the job; so be sure to include the listing of accomplishments or qualifications to impress the person reading your resume.

The credentials section should include academic and technical education and training. You may also wish to include certificate programs and certifications. If appropriate, list licenses or professional accreditations. The important consideration is to include only those credentials that are pertinent

---

PROFESSIONAL EXPERIENCE

| March 2000–Present | **Food & Beverage Manager, Hotel California, Key West, FL**
Senior manager responsible for the operation of three food and beverage outlets at an exclusive boutique luxury resort.

• Restructured management team to improve efficiency and effectiveness.

• Significantly increased average check rates in all outlets.

• Established thorough training programs in steps of service and product knowledge, resulting in much higher ratings on guest service index scores.

• Continue to enhance productivity on a daily basis. |

Figure 11–3.   Sample career summary position description.

to the job. For example, an individual applying for a sales position with a cruise line should not include a real estate license on the resume. Why? The reader may conclude that this person may leave the position within a short time to pursue real estate sales. While this may not be the person's intention, listing the license may give the wrong impression. More important is the question, "Does listing this qualification help me look qualified for this specific position?" In this case, listing the real estate license doesn't help and may hurt the candidate's chances of getting the preliminary interview.

Some people work in two or more different fields. For instance, a person may hold an executive-level position and teach college part time. Or a person may work days in a hospitality or retail position and work nights as a musician. In these cases, individuals would want to establish two resumes, one for each area of work.

Some people choose to include affiliations in the credentials section. Sales people, for instance, may want to list professional associations in which they hold memberships. For a sales position, this is appropriate, as the potential employer would look favorably on the networking activities of a sales representative. However, if an affiliation does not enhance your qualifications for the position, you may want to exclude it from the resume. For instance, a person applying for an employment counseling position need not include the fact that she belongs to the National Rifle Association. On the other hand, club memberships that demonstrate leadership or management ability may help a person seeking a supervisor's position for the first time. A sample credentials section is shown in Figure 11.4.

Notice the use of bold lettering. Also, there is a section heading, with subheadings on the left side of each subsection. Educational degrees should be listed in descending order. Also, notice there is no date of graduation listed for the bachelor degree. This information may not enhance the qualifications of the candidate. Graduation dates may encourage the reader to speculate about the age of the applicant. This, of course, is not information that is relevant to the job. Therefore, dates of graduation should be omitted in most cases. Individuals who plan to graduate from an academic program in a short period of time may want to list the degree with the date of intended completion. (Notice the date given for the master's degree in the figure.)

Another alternative for students who have not yet completed a degree program would be to list the intended degree with the word "Candidate" next to it.

	EDUCATION, MEMBERSHIPS & HONORS
EDUCATION	**University of Central Florida, Rosen School of Hospitality Management—Orlando, Florida**
	M.S. Hospitality and Tourism Management (2004)
	B.S. Hospitality Management, Convention Management Emphasis
MEMBERSHIPS & HONORS	Hospitality Association, President (2003), Student Professional Organization
	Society of Human Resource Management (SHRM)
	Certified Manager (CM), Institute of Certified Professional Managers (ICPM)

Figure 11–4. Sample credentials section.

It should be noted that, while many employers do not take the time to check on college degrees and high school diplomas, this information is very easy to verify. Therefore, job seekers should be cautioned to avoid listing any credentials that they don't have. This could cost the individual his job or hurt his reputation. As a matter of ethics, all information on any document should be true to the best knowledge of the person preparing the document.

Many individuals choose to include personal information such as hobbies, marital status, parental status, religious/political affiliations, age, self-help activities, and mental rehabilitation programs. It is recommended that personal information be excluded from the resume. Remember, for each item listed on the resume, ask two questions: first, "How can this information help me get an interview?" and second, "How could this information be used to exclude me from getting an interview?" A general rule of thumb is to provide only job-related information.

A cover letter should be composed and sent with your resume. The cover letter should be somewhat personalized. Therefore, we recommend using software that will permit you to modify cover letters to suit the job search situation and the company. The letter should sell you and your skills to the prospective employer for the particular job sought. It should be brief (three paragraphs are recommended) and fit on one sheet of paper. The preferred style for the cover letter is block format, which uses left and right justification to the margins. This is the writing style used for most business correspondence.

HOSPITALITY TIPS & CLIPS   *It's Time to Start a Career Portfolio*

Editor's note: Following are excerpts taken from a Hospitality News *interview with Anna Graf Williams, Ph.D., author of* Creating Your Career Portfolio—At a Glance Guide.

Q. Briefly explain what a career portfolio contains.

A. A career portfolio is an organized set of work samples. It should also contain your work philosophy, goals, resume, community service activities, as well as any degrees or certifications you have achieved.

Q. What is the benefit of having a career portfolio?

A. Resumes get you the interview, but career portfolios can get you the job. It can prove to a potential employer that you have the skills to complete the job at hand. Your portfolio will give you a competitive edge, compared to the other candidates.

Q. Putting together a career portfolio sounds a little overwhelming, any advice as to how to get it started?

A. I teach students to collect it now and sort it later. Start saving samples of class assignments or things you've developed on the job. For example, if you created a menu for a special event—save that. If you organized the table layout at a banquet—take a photo and save it. As you gain experience, ask for letters of referral and save them.

When you put together your portfolio, you'll need to sort through what you've collected. You won't want to include everything; be selective and include the collateral that will best reflect where you're wanting to go with your career.

Q. How do you use a career portfolio during a job interview?

A. There are three ways to use it. First, bring it with you to the interview and say, " I have my career portfolio with me, would you like to see it?" Then go through it and point out the significant pieces that most relate to the job you are seeking. Secondly, have your portfolio on your lap and use it to answer questions. For instance, if you are asked what experience you've had leading others, you can open your portfolio and show that you were president of a club at school, and you also have a letter from a boss praising you for organizing a company party—these real-life examples will show proof of your abilities. This gives you added confidence as you answer questions. Finally, you can offer to leave your career portfolio for 24 hours with the interviewer. This will give him/her the opportunity to carefully look through it and give you the chance to be in contact with the interviewer one additional time. Some students are doing an electronic portfolio and putting it on disk which they can leave with the potential employer.

Q. How do most employers react to a career portfolio?

A. The typical reaction is, "Wow, you have made my job so much easier! I wish everyone would do this!" Basically, the feedback we get is that employers love it.

Q. Once you've landed a job, what should you do with your career portfolio?

A. Now your portfolio can help you build your career. Continue to keep letters and performance appraisals, photos of events you've been involved in, etc. As you go into a performance review you can take your portfolio with you, or better yet, give it to your supervisor a week to 10 days prior to your meeting. The portfolio will serve as a reminder of some of your job accomplishments and will help your supervisors as they evaluate you.

Source: Interview with Anna G. Williams. "It's Time to Start a Career Portfolio." *Hospitality News* 2, no. 2 (Fall 2002): p. 2. Courtesy of *Hospitality News.*

Job Search Prospecting

A job search is an endeavor that requires a high level of commitment on the part of the searcher. Job searchers who are between jobs (a euphemism for unemployed) should consider the job search to be their full-time job. Thus, the search is their major activity for at least 8 hours a day. The currently employed or student job searcher should devote every free moment to job search activities.

Job searches require large amounts of energy. The reason for this is that job searchers (without exception) experience multiple forms of rejection. Phone calls and emails are not returned, responses are not received, impersonal rejection letters and postcards are found in the mail. These experiences are depressing. Also, they drain the energy of the job searcher. Job searchers are encouraged to use stress management techniques to replenish depleted energy levels, maintain self-esteem, and renew their enthusiasm for the search on a daily basis.

This section considers prospecting activities. Many of you remember this term from sales or marketing courses. When you conduct a job search, you are a salesperson. The product consists of the knowledge and skills that you will bring to an organization. The purpose of prospecting is to generate leads. In the case of a job search, a lead is any person who may influence (directly or indirectly) a decision to let you bid for a job. The purpose of prospecting is to generate as many qualified leads as possible. The more leads you generate, the more opportunities you have to close at least one sale (in this case a job offer).

The majority of job searchers rely primarily on newspaper classified employment advertisements to generate leads on position opportunities. While this is perhaps the most commonly used technique for announcing job openings, it is the least reliable type of lead available to the job searcher. Advertisements are usually placed for hard-to-fill or commonly replaced positions. By the time an advertisement is placed, at least 3 days have passed since members of the hiring organization have noticed the vacancy. Also, advertisements are usually contracted to run for a number of consecutive days, due to the pricing structure for classified ads. That means that you may be reading an ad that has been running for 5 days. In such cases (especially if the position is attractive), the hiring people for that organization have been deluged with stacks of resumes. Another factor concerning responding to classified ads is that they are impersonal. You are just another unknown stranger among many who have expressed an interest in an employment opportunity. Finally, there are motives other than filling positions that encourage organizations to run advertisements. Company policy, equal employment requirements, and affirmative action programs cause companies to run ads, even after a position has been filled. This is not to say that classified advertisements are not a bona fide source for job searches; it is simply that the chances of rejection are much higher for respondents to classified ads than other forms of job search prospecting

There are those whose profession is to assist individuals with finding jobs. These include executive search firms ("headhunters"), employment agencies, out-placement services, electronic employment bulletin boards, and college placement services. Some of these agents charge fees for job placement. In many cases the employer pays those fees. However, there are agen-

---

HOSPITALITY TIPS & CLIPS   *Don't Look for a Job—Create a Position*

There is a distinct difference between a person who wants a job and one who wants to create a position for himself. Job seekers are primarily concerned about how much they will earn. Job seekers think the best place to find a job is in the want ads of the local newspapers. Most job seekers take the first job available and are quick to quit a job when the going gets tough.

On the other hand, those who seek to create a position usually are following a passion and aren't afraid to talk to everyone they can find with similar interests. Networking comes easily to the job creator. These individuals care about a meaningful work life and will often find an opportunity where none really existed. In other words, they create opportunities for themselves. They believe in themselves and can find a way to show that their skills and talents will assist a company. Those who create their positions use job experiences and contacts to create their next opportunity and never burn bridges with previous employers.

Source: "Don't Look for a Job—Create a Position." *Hospitality News* 1, no.1 (Fall 2001): p. 26. Courtesy of *Hospitality News.*

---

cies that charge the applicant fees that are sometimes very expensive. It is recommended that job searchers avoid dealing with agencies that charge the job searcher a placement or prospecting fee. Many times these agencies have you pay to get a job that you could get by yourself.

The best form of prospecting is to establish job search leads through personal networking activities. Personal networking may include direct contact with hiring officials or other members of the hiring organization. These are direct leads. Personal networking may also include referrals from respected individuals outside the hiring organization. The advantage of personal networking (direct or indirect) is that the job searcher is getting a personalized introduction to someone involved in the hiring process or, at least, is able to call a member of the hiring organization and use the name of someone who is known to that person. This provides a personal flavor of familiarity.

One of the drawbacks of responding to advertisements is that the respondent is not a "real person" in the mind of the reader. Instead, the job searcher is just a printed name on a page. With a personal introduction, you establish rapport with the representative of the hiring organization because you have someone or something in common. You are more likely to be able to schedule a meeting with this type of rapport. This is because the hiring person recognizes you as a real person whom she has met or who was referred by "good ole So-and-So" from X corporation.

Job searchers are encouraged to construct a prospecting plan at the beginning of the job search. Networking activities could include, for example, five calls per day to acquaintances, college professors, classmates, former work colleagues, friends, members of associations or clubs, relatives, or any person who may be able to direct you to someone seeking to fill a position.

HOSPITALITY TIPS & CLIPS *Look to the Internet As You Grow Your Hospitality Career*

The Internet is a tremendous resource for those looking for positions in the hospitality industry. Here are a few websites that might be a good place to start your search.

www.restaurant.org The official website of the National Restaurant Association, this site includes resources for education and career development, food safety, industry events, etc.

www.nraef.org The National Restaurant Association Education Foundation's website offers students and professionals a host of resources to enhance their careers. This website also includes a listing of scholarship opportunities.

www.hcareers.com The National Restaurant Association has recently endorsed this website, which lists job openings throughout North America and the United Kingdom. The site accommodates both those searching for jobs as well as those employers seeking qualified workers. This site also gives you the opportunity to post your resume for future openings.

www.acfchefs.org The American Culinary Federation is a national organization for culinary professionals. This website offers information about apprenticeship and professional development opportunities.

www.chrie.org The Council on International, Hotel, Restaurant and Institutional Education is made up of professional hospitality educators. The organization's website provides links to various teaching opportunities at different hospitality programs. It also includes information about CHRIE's publications as well as links to the group's European chapter.

www.bls.gov/oco/ This U.S. government website gives a comprehensive guide to employment prospects in every possible career field and offers general job information such as starting pay, working conditions, and so on.

Additional sites of interest:

www.hmcareers.com
www.hsmai.org
www.hotelinteractive.com
www.lodgingnews.com
www.culinaryconnect.com
www.winealley.com
www.foodonline.com
www.site-intl.org
www.hotel-publication.com
www.worldhospitality.com
www.TourismWorkWeb.com
www.meetingsquest.com
www.culinarysoftware.com
www.gelighting.com
www.ntfonline.com
www.hospitality-1st.com
www.fastweb.com

Source: "Look to the Internet As You Grow Your Hospitality Career." *Hospitality News* 2, no. 2 (Fall 2002): p.12. Courtesy of *Hospitality News*.

Professional Image

Most companies preach hance to provide a first impression. Every aspect of the job search process provides opportunities for others to evaluate the job searcher from the context of image. The job searcher's personal appearance and the appearance of his written documents will create an image perception in the minds of hiring decision makers.

As stated earlier, all correspondence (resumes, letters, etc.) should be neat and orderly. Edit for typographical errors, misspellings, and improper grammar. Use quality paper that is bright white and free of stains and tatters. Be sure that print is appropriately dark with easy-to-read fonts.

Telephone etiquette is another factor influencing perceptions of image. For instance, if a job searcher is expecting returned phone calls to her home, it may be time to disconnect the Austin Powers voice mail message. A major mistake made by senior-level job searchers is the way they treat reception and assistant personnel who answer the phone. Many times they will not validate the phone answerer as a person by failing to say "good morning" or "hello." Instead they may bark, "George Jetson, please." The job searcher is also failing to develop rapport with the phone answerer. By doing this, the job searcher is damaging his image. This is a big mistake, as administrative personnel have the ability to influence hiring executives' opinions concerning job candidates.

A final factor that influences image is appearance. Appearance includes grooming, hygiene, and attire. Other image factors are posture, use of space, hand gestures, eye contact, and speech. Numerous publications address these issues and offer advice for creating powerful perceptions through projecting a positive image. Books and audiotapes on this topic are available at most bookstores.

Interviewing

Congratulations! You have successfully composed a resume and cover letter, done some effective prospecting, and created a positive image.

While there are plenty of sources to provide information on effective interviewing, the one ingredient that is crucial is *practice*. You may practice by participating in actual interviews, conducting videotaped roleplays, or even rehearsing in front of a mirror.

The factors that influence image perception apply to the interview. The first consideration is to create an appropriate appearance. Well-groomed and dressed for success are the key factors here. Hair should be worn in a conservative manner. Conservatism also applies to jewelry, makeup, and style of dress.

Standard business attire should be worn at the interview. It is recommended that interviewees wear dark colors (blue, gray, black) with contrasting ties, scarves, and handkerchiefs. Clothes should be clean and crisp. The interviewee should carry a small briefcase or leather-bound folder containing reference lists, other pertinent documents, and a list of prepared questions to ask at the end of the interview (if invited to do so).

A final consideration during the interview is conduct. It is likely that there will be a period of time in which the interviewee may be asked to wait in a reception area (hopefully for a short period of time). Keep in mind that you may be under observation during your wait. When you finally get to meet the interviewer, greet her with a firm handshake and sincere gestures. When seated, assume an erect but relaxed posture. Lean slightly toward the interviewer and make frequent eye contact (do not stare). Listen actively to what the interviewer says and paraphrase for understanding when appropriate. Try to speak at the same rate and tone of speech as that used by the interviewer. For instance, if the interviewer speaks quickly and in a monotone, try to match that rate with your own speech.

Prior to the interview, you should have done some research on the company and the position. You should also have prepared a list of questions. As

HOSPITALITY TIPS & CLIPS   *Ten Tips for Successful Job Interviews*

Whether you're a recent graduate or just wanting to gain a little work experience as you continue your education, the skills that you should use during job interviews are primarily the same. Following are 10 tips that will help you as you interview for jobs.

Tip #1   Always do your homework. Go to the interview knowing a little about the company and the position (check out their website or call ahead and ask questions of the receptionist). Don't waste your time or the interviewer's by trying for jobs for which you are not qualified.

Tip #2   Arrive at the interview 10 to 15 minutes early. If you are unfamiliar with the location, do a practice run a day or two ahead of the interview.

Tip #3   Dress appropriately. As a rule of thumb, wear the level of dress that you will be asked to wear for the position, although it's better to be overdressed than to dress too casually. Be sure to dress conservatively. Leave the fad jewelry at home.

Tip #4   Speak slowly and clearly and with enough volume to be heard.

Tip #5   Don't forget to smile and look the interviewer in the eyes. Don't look down. Your head up and shoulders back shows that you have some pride in yourself. Keep hands resting comfortably at your side while standing or folded in your lap while seated.

Tip #6   Offer a handshake when greeting your interviewer and again prior to departing.

Tip #7   Have a resume or application neatly filled out and ready to offer the interviewer.

Tip #8   Show your interest as the interviewer describes the position and company information to you. Don't be afraid to ask questions about the company.

Tip #9   Don't be afraid to "sell" yourself. Make the interviewer truly believe that you want this position more than any other on earth.

Tip #10   Follow up your interview by sending a thank-you note to your interviewer. Reiterate your interest in the position and your ability to fulfill the job requirements.

Source: "Ten Tips for Successful Job Interviews." *Hospitality News* 1, no. 1 (Fall 2001): p. 34. Courtesy of *Hospitality News*.

the interview draws to a close, the interviewer may ask if there are any questions about the position or the organization. Be sure to exclude any prepared questions that have already been answered during the interview process. Be sure to ask (if it hasn't been stated) what you may expect as far as further contact. If appropriate, ask the interviewer when you may place a follow-up call or email. Memorize the interviewer's full name or ask for a business card. Thank the interviewer for her time. Follow up with a thank-you letter, card, or email.

SUMMARY

This chapter has presented future supervisors with basic tips on conducting an effective job search. Emphasis has been placed on planning, resume writing, prospecting activities, and interviewing.

The job search is a ritual that all of us experience at various times during our careers. The search can be a grueling process. Energy conservation, planning, and implementation of strategies are crucial to conducting an effective and efficient search.

Readers are encouraged to seek sources of information that are available concerning the various aspects of a job search. Through knowledge and practice, the job search process will become easier to conduct over time. This set of skills will contribute to your successful career progression.

ENDNOTE

1. Martin Yate, *Resumes That Knock'Em Dead* (Avon, MA: Adams Media Corp, 2000).

... In the Real World (Continued)

As it turns out, you have decided not to go to work at any of your former places of employment. During your last semester at school you attended a few job fairs, networked with some industry professionals, and developed some wonderful references.

A recruiter for a cruise line got your name from one of your professors who used to work in that industry, and they are willing to hire you in a shore-side marketing position at their central office. The job pays well, with great benefits that include free travel. Sometimes the job leads just come from the most unexpected places.

CHAPTER TWELVE
Putting It All Together

OBJECTIVE

At the end of this chapter, readers will be able to:

1. Use the tools in this book to navigate a scenario as a newly appointed supervisor.

You now have all of the tools required to operate as an effective and efficient supervisor. You may recall that effectiveness involves providing quality services and efficiency is the ability to maximize the use of resources that results in lower expenses. Since we understand the concepts of effectiveness and efficiency, we are value-added supervisors, because these two concepts contribute to enhancing productivity every day. But this may be too much, too soon for this discussion.

As one well-known author suggests, let's "begin with the end in mind."[1] The last chapter was all about getting a job or a promotion. Congratulations, you are now a supervisor based on your efforts in the areas of resume and letter writing, prospecting, networking, and effective interviewing. If you were hired as the first supervisor in a new department or organization, you would build your department from "scratch," using each chapter of this book in succession. However, it is unlikely that this is the case for a first-time supervisor. Chances are you are inheriting a department from a prior supervisor and have to figure out how to run it from this point forward. We call this "organizational inheritance tax," in which the problems of the past are inherited by the present supervisor. Whenever this is the case, we advise working through the book backwards from getting the job back through the development of a service perspective. We know we want to achieve the type of performance articulated in the first chapter (the "end" we seek), but we also know we must work through the process of "what is" to determine how to make it "what it should be." Let's assume for the purpose of this chapter that you have inherited a marginally performing department. That is to say, the department you are now supervising is not terrible, but it may be one that is not too good in terms of potential performance. From this assumption you begin your intervention as the new supervisor.

MEASURING PERFORMANCE

The first activity for you as the new supervisor is to assess the operation of the department. This will include an appraisal of current performance levels among all the staff members (employees). You would probably seek a documented version of the standards for performance to use as your benchmark. Unfortunately, you may find that no such document exists. Now what? Well, since you embody a *service perspective*, you have a good idea of what service performance should look like. So, you engage in conversations with individual members of the staff to determine their ideas of good service, how they have been rated for performance in the past, what they think will improve service, and so on. It is very likely that some individuals may not tell you the truth. With this in mind, you seek patterns of opinions among all the workers in the department.

At the same time, you are observing performance levels. Is what the workers do the same as what they told you, or is there a difference? Do your observations meet with your concept of the service perspective? Do they fall short; exceed it, perhaps? Do the staff members willingly assist each other? Are there some very good performers and a few that are not so good, in your opinion? Are the guests or customers "wowed" by the service? Satisfied? Dissatisfied? Complacent? How are sales? Are some staff members turning in

---

HOSPITALITY TIPS & CLIPS *Beyond Yesterday's Basics*

Reading, writing, and arithmetic used to be considered the basics of education. But the jobs of tomorrow, while still requiring these essential skills, will also require a new set of workplace skills, according to a study by the American Society for Training and Development, a professional organization of corporate trainers.

- **Creative thinking.** As work becomes more flexible, workers' solutions will need to become more creative.
- **Goal setting/motivation.** Workers will need to be able to set objectives and persist in achieving them.
- **Interpersonal skills.** Being able to get along with suppliers, coworkers, and customers will be essential in future work.
- **Leadership.** Workers will be asked to assume more responsibility and direct their coworkers when needed.
- **Learning to learn.** Workers will need to learn new information and develop new skills, and be able to apply the new information and skills to their jobs.
- **Listening.** Good listening skills will help workers understand the concerns of coworkers, suppliers, and customers.

- **Negotiation.** Workers should be able to build agreement through give-and-take negotiating.
- **Oral communications.** Workers must be able to respond clearly to the concerns of coworkers, suppliers, and customers.
- **Organizational effectiveness.** Employees will need to understand how the company's business goals are met and how their jobs contribute to fulfilling those goals.
- **Personal/career development skills.** The most valuable employees will be those who understand that they need to continually develop new skills on the job.
- **Problem solving.** Workers will be asked to find answers and solve problems.
- **Self-esteem.** Supervisors say they want (and expect) workers who are proud of themselves and their abilities.
- **Teamwork.** Working cooperatively means workers must effectively and equitably divide work to achieve team goals.

Source: "Beyond Yesterday's Basics." *Hospitality News* (August 2002): p. 33. Courtesy of *Hospitality News.*

---

high average sales per customer, while others are not? Is there a correlation with employee discussions among high-sales-volume people versus lower-volume sellers? Do some staff members arrive 10 minutes or so early for each shift, while others have a tendency to be a little late? Do the early ones seem to perform better than the late ones? These are just some of the questions you may be asking yourself as a new supervisor who is observing performance and having individual discussions with the staff. Naturally, you would use the critical incident method to record your observations and frequently review those notes to identify performance patterns.

BUILDING TEAMS

A novice supervisor might begin with team-building activities immediately upon being assigned to the position. This is not the case with you. You know that team building is reserved for some point in the future when the department is operating at a higher level. You do, however, make note of the team critical incidents you observe while assessing the staff's performance. You notice those who willingly help others and those who take advantage of their coworkers. You make note of cliques that may exist among the workers. Are some of them informal leaders? If so, do they provide constructive or destructive influence over their coworkers? Are some of the staff members accustomed to receiving preferential treatment over the others? If so—do they deserve special favors based on their performance, or did the former supervisor just have personal favorites for whatever reasons? Do you see potential for building a team among the current workers, or will some of them never contribute to a synergistic work environment in the future?

These and other notes are recorded in your critical incident file for future reference when team-building activities may be warranted. These observations will also assist you in determining which staff members to invest your energy in working with at the present time, as well as those who don't seem to deserve that kind of attention.

EMPLOYEE COUNSELING AND DISCIPLINE

As you continue with your overall assessment of the operation, you may want to review the personnel files for each of the staff members in your work unit. These files would be located in the human resources office, and you are entitled to review them at any time. The files should contain documentation regarding the performance of the staff members, to include counseling sessions, disciplinary warnings, commendation letters, and recognition documents. As you review this information compare the documentation to your own observations in the department. Are those who seem to perform well recognized appropriately in their files? How about those who don't perform well? Are there indications of counseling and warnings in the files for those individuals? If the information in the files does not match your observations, there may have been subjective management practices on the part of a former supervisor. If the documentation is consistent with your observations, then you may assume that the files reflect actual performance levels for workers in your unit.

In some cases the operation may be small and no human resources office may be in place. Hopefully, there will be a secured location for personnel files in this type of operation. In the event that this is not the case, you will be placed in a position to start fresh by establishing a file for each worker in the department. You will want to keep those files in a very secure area to preclude access by unauthorized individuals. In this case, you have no documented history concerning staff member performance, which means you will have to start recording performance levels from this point forward.

If the organization has a counseling and discipline policy, you will want to familiarize yourself with it and follow it to the letter. In the absence of a policy, you should establish one in the near future. This also applies to complaint and grievance procedures in your work unit.

COMPLAINTS AND GRIEVANCES

While it is always important to actively listen to those workers who perceive unfair treatment in the workplace, this is a crucial time for this activity. There are two reasons for this. First, you are making an initial impression on the

staff members in the department and it is important for them to perceive you as a fair and concerned supervisor. Second, you are in assessment mode, and complaints or grievances will provide you with additional insight to the thoughts and perceptions of the workers.

You may observe that the lower-level performers lodge the largest amounts of complaints. There may be a number of reasons for this. It could be that they are attempting to cover up their poor performance by blaming others for their circumstances. Or they could be trying to divert your attention from the matter at hand, which very simply is departmental performance. Finally, they may just need help in the form of training or support of some sort. Regardless of the legitimacy of their vocalizations, you must indicate your interest in their welfare by validating them while hearing what they have to say. The time for training and such will come in the near future.

EMPLOYEE TRAINING

By now you have probably determined the levels of training that have been available to the staff members. You may be pleasantly surprised to find a cache of well-prepared training programs to provide technical skills for the staff. On the other hand, you may discover that there has been no training whatsoever, or maybe something in between the two scenarios. Whether there is evidence of prior training or not, you probably have determined by now through your observations who needs additional training. You have done this by asking, do they perform poorly because they don't know how or because they don't want to perform well? If they don't know how to perform but want to perform well, then you have a learning gap, which means you will place those individuals in training mode once you have completed your assessment of the department.

SUPERVISORY COMMUNICATION

Throughout your assessment activities you have been communicating both verbally and nonverbally with the members of the staff. They have watched you closely and are beginning to formulate an opinion of who you are in terms of your supervisory style.

On a verbal level, you have interacted with them in the course of operations by assisting them with their work activities and perhaps showing them a trick or two along the way. Also, you have had individual discussions with them concerning their perception of the operation and their role as staff members in the work unit. Finally, you have actively listened to their concerns via complaints and grievances that may have arisen. While you have had a busy period of verbal interaction, the perceptions of the workers have been most influenced by those nonverbal cues you have been sending out.

The nonverbal cues articulate who you are without uttering a single syllable. The perceptions of professionalism come from the way you walk, how you dress, your general demeanor, posture, and approach with guests, customers, and the staff. Your work ethic has been demonstrated by the things you do: the types of work you engage in, how active you are during the course of business, the hours you work, the fact that you choose to arrive early and leave the work site late. Through these activities you have demonstrated that you would not ask a staff member to perform any activity that you would not do yourself. Standards for performance are emphasized by the way you yourself handle interactions with guests and customers. These are being communicated before you have committed them to written and verbal communication media. In just one week or so, the future direction of the work unit has been made clear before you have formalized your plan for supervising the staff.

EMPLOYEE MOTIVATION AND LEADERSHIP

Based on your observations, discussions, review of documents, and general intuition, you probably have a pretty good idea of the emotional "switches" that ignite the passion in each of the staff members. You know which ones are motivated by money, attention, recognition, consequence avoidance, autonomy, status, and achievement. You have a mental profile for each worker based on his motivational preferences. You also have an idea of the type of leadership style that will suit the situation in the department. Maybe you will choose to be task oriented with some of the staff members and relations oriented with others. You may choose to micro-manage those who want your attention and delegate to those who seek autonomy. Perhaps you will identify an informal leader who influences others in a constructive manner and promote her to the level of "key" employee to satisfy her need for achievement. This will become the core of your power to influence the staff members in your work unit to willingly meet your standards for performance and ultimately collaborate as future team players to create synergistic outcomes for the department. If you choose to lead these people the way they want to be led, you will gain the most influential power base, called "referent power."

CAREER DEVELOPMENT THROUGH PERSONAL TRANSFORMATION

Based on your observations and discussions, where are your staff members in the course of their careers? Chances are some of them are with your work unit temporarily, others are there for a longer duration, and some are goal oriented, while others may not be sure what lies ahead for their careers. Soon it will be time for you to identify your own successor and start to groom that person to fill your position. Why would you want to do this? Because when you have a "person in the pocket" you are preparing yourself for the next promotional opportunity that comes your way. However, this is premature speculation on your part, but something that should be in the back of your mind. For now, let's begin at the beginning to rebuild this work unit by starting with the development of a service perspective.

A SERVICE PERSPECTIVE

You have already set the tone through your interactions and behaviors. Now, it is time to formalize the supervision practices for the department. In other words, it is time to "plan your work and work your plan." At this point it is time for you to become strategic in your supervisory approach. With the service perspective in mind and knowing the overall mission for the organization, you will determine your mission and objectives for your work unit. Once those are in place, you will be ready to establish tactics to accomplish your objectives.

The first tactic will be to establish policies, standards, and procedures for performance in your work area. You will formalize these in a document that may be called "Steps of Service" or "Standard Operating Procedures." Notice that this is the first part of your communication strategy to document established standards and procedures for performance to be communicated to the staff. Additional communication strategies will be procedures for meetings, memos, emails, and other forms of communication for the purpose of sharing information and exchanging ideas to enhance performance in the work unit.

Did you identify a learning gap during your assessment? Do you want to be sure that new staff members become prepared to meet your newly established standards and procedures? Well, if you weren't lucky enough to find all those great training programs, it looks like you will have to develop them. This will come in handy for those staff members you observed who want to perform well but just don't know how to do it. And those constructive informal leaders you noticed—they might be candidates to help you train new and existing staff members, especially if they are motivated by status or achievement. Obviously, this is your second communication strategy.

While you are in formal communication mode, why not establish procedures for complaints and grievances, as well as counseling and discipline? This will facilitate clear expectations for your staff members about your open door policy and what to expect in the event of poor performance or misconduct. Of course, to keep things balanced you may want to outline a procedure for recognizing those excellent workers in your unit and communicate that to the staff as well.

So far, you have established a mission, objectives, tactics, policies, standards, and procedures for performance. To support these, you have developed procedures for training, complaints, and grievances, as well as counseling and discipline practices. With this foundation in place, it should be time for you to develop teams within your work unit. Remember those willing helpers and constructive informal leaders you observed in your first couple of weeks on the job? These staff members will probably become your team leaders. One of them will likely surface as the ideal candidate for you to train as your replacement.

Now, let's fast-forward a little bit in time. It has been about 1 year since you took over the operation. You worked hard to put things in order during the first 3 months. But soon after, your job became progressively easier. Now there are open and effective communication channels in your work unit. All of the employees have been thoroughly trained, and your designated trainer handles all new hires. Complaints and grievances are exceptions these days as opposed to being the norm when you first took charge. The same is true for counseling and discipline activities. As a matter of fact, most entries to personnel files lately have been recognition certificates and letters of appreciation for the services provided by your excellent staff. Because of the wonderful reputation of your department, you have a waiting list of employee transfer requests to work in your area, should a position become available. All in all, your job is easy. You simply work smarter, not harder, as do all the members of your staff, thanks to your leadership.

Because you are running one of the most productive work units in the organization, you are being considered for a promotion to a higher-level management position. Fortunately, your key employee knows almost as much about running the department as you do. The decision makers for your new position are impressed when they find out you have a fully qualified replacement for your current job, should you get the promotion. This gives you an edge over the other candidates.

SUMMARY

Congratulations! You are well on your way to career development through your own personal transformation.

Each chapter in this book has been like a rung on a ladder. In a new department or organization, you start at the top of the ladder and work your way down to developing a successful operation. If you inherit an existing department, you start at the bottom of the ladder and work your way to the top during the departmental assessment phase. Then you descend the ladder while building each component of the supervision process one rung at a time. When you reach the bottom of that ladder, your work unit is on its way to excellent guest and customer service while continually enhancing productivity. In other words, you become a successful supervisor. And quite simply, that is—*How to Do It!*

ENDNOTE

1. S. R. Covey. *The 7 Habits of Highly Effective People.* New York: Simon & Schuster.

Glossary

Advancement stage—The stage in the Work Life Development Model in which individuals are seeking higher-level positions of authority and responsibility.

Assimilation stage—The first stage in the Work Life Development Model in which individuals become accustomed to performing in full-time positions with organizations.

Behavioral modification theory—A process theory of motivation based on a system of behaviors and consequences that contain stimulus and response relationships, in the forms of reinforcing desired behaviors and punishing negative behaviors.

Change agentry—The activity of implementing methodical change strategies.

Channel—The directional flow of communications.

Coaching—Working with individuals to progressively develop their skills and habits.

Communication—The process of exchanging ideas for the purpose of sharing information and concepts.

Competence—The ability to function effectively and efficiently in a position.

Complaint—The communication of dissatisfaction with a situation.

Conflict—Differences of ideology demonstrated through interactive behaviors.

Counseling—Providing advice for the welfare of an individual.

Critical incident method—A method for recording and recalling observable behaviors that are important aspects of worker performance.

Critical shift—A major change in attitudes, values, and beliefs for an individual.

Critical tasks—Those activities that contribute to the mission for an organization.

Crucial tasks—Those tasks that must be performed immediately to avoid some sort of negative consequence.

Decode—To mentally comprehend a message sent by a sender in the communication process.

Discharge—Involuntary separation from an organization.

Discipline—Redirecting behaviors to achieve the objectives of an organization.

Duration—The length of interactive time spent with customers in an organization.

Effectiveness—Generating outputs that meet standards for quality and quantity.

Efficiency—Procuring and using resources in a way that minimizes the cost of inputs.

Empathy—Personal identification with the emotions felt by another individual.

Employee turnover—The number of workers who separate from positions in an organization and require replacement.

Encode—To convert an idea into symbols for communication to a receiver in the communication process.

Equity theory—A process theory of motivation based on the perception of fairness among individuals in a work unit or organization.

Expectancy theory—A process theory of motivation based on the perceived value and probability of attaining a reward for performance.

External customers—Those individuals who choose to purchase products and services from an organization.

Feedback—The process of reinforcing awareness of an interactive activity.

Formal leader—An individual appointed by an organization to a position of responsibility with the authority to delegate tasks.

Goals—The targets for performance in an organization; objectives.

Grapevine—A form of informal communication that includes activities such as gossip or rumors.

Grievance—A complaint received from a worker about perceived unfair treatment in the organization.

Gross misconduct—A violation of the rules for behavior in an organization that warrants immediate employee discharge.

Hierarchy of needs theory—A content theory of motivation that suggests a scale of individual needs from lowest to highest.

Influence stage—The stage in the Work Life Development Model in which an individual is in a position to serve as a role model to others.

Informal leader—An individual with the ability to influence others within an organization absent a position of authority to delegate tasks.

Input—The supply of resources infused into a transformation process to yield outputs.

Integration stage—The stage in the Work Life Development Model in which an individual chooses to function in a state of values-based balance.

Interdependent state—A mental state of balanced interactivity of give-and-take, in which an individual or subsystem is not controlled by nor isolated from a system.

Internal customers—Workers within an organization who use the products and services of other workers to interact with external customers.

Intimacy level—The level of personal interaction with a customer in the process of providing products and services.

"It depends. . ."—A standard response from one worker to another in an organization to indicate that the situation or environment is the determining influence on making optimal decisions.

Job enlargement—Adding tasks to the existing job list for an individual worker.

Job enrichment—Adding authority and autonomy along with enhanced responsibility to the job list for an individual worker.

Job rotation—Moving an individual worker to different positions requiring varying tasks.

KSAAs—Knowledge, skills, attitudes, and abilities to perform the tasks, duties, and responsibilities of a position within an organization in a productive manner.

Knowledge—The information possessed by an individual.

Leadership—The demonstrated ability to influence others to willingly participate in activities.

Learning—The process of enacting permanent change within an individual.

Line worker—A worker who interacts directly with customers and/or generates revenue for an organization.

Machiavelli—Author of *The Prince,* who suggested that leaders are born, not made.

Management by objectives—Top/down and bottom/ up goal-setting that are planning and performance evaluation tools used in participative organizations.

Meaning system—Performance drivers that include mission, vision, philosophy, values, and beliefs of people within an organization.

Medium—The mechanism used to carry a message through a channel in the communication process.

Mission—The philosophy that explains the purpose of existence of an organization.

Motivation—The willingness that creates intentions for behavior among individuals and groups.

Negative reinforcement—Removing an unpleasant experience as a reward for desired behavior.

Objectives—Targets for performance; goals.

Open door policy—The availability of the supervisor to discuss concerns of the workers within an organization.

Organizational culture—Shared values, attitudes, and beliefs among workers in an organization.

Output—The products and services produced within an organization.

Performance assessment—A comparison of actual performance to standards for performance; performance evaluation.

Performance management system—A system of expectations, training, and assessment of performance for workers in an organization.

Personality traits—A person's preference for behavior given certain environmental stimuli. Considered to be both genetic and learned, it compromises a person's social comfort zone.

Policies—Broad guidelines for performance in an organization.

Positive reinforcement—Initiating a pleasant experience as a reward for desired behavior.

Proactive approach—Strategic thinking used to prevent problems from occurring.

Problem—A negative gap between standards for performance and actual performance.

Problem employees—Individuals employed by an organization who exhibit chronic behaviors deemed to be destructive to the performance of a work unit.

Procedures—The listing of tasks that result in meeting standards for performance.

Productivity—Adding value to the organization through reducing costs of resources and enhancing the quantity and quality of outputs.

Receiver—The intended recipient of a message in the communication process.

Retirement stage—The stage in the Work Life Development Model in which individuals stop contributing to an organization after a long period of service.

Sender—The person with an idea who wants to send a message to someone else.

Situation—The environment in an organization at a given time.

Skills—Those demonstrated abilities of workers to contribute to the production of products and services in an organization.

Staff worker—A worker who advises or supports a line worker in an organization.

Stakeholders—Constituency groups of an organization (customers, employees, shareholders, and the community).

Standards—The expectations for performance in an organization.

Stewardship—Willing service to ensure the welfare of constituents.

Strategies—Action steps implemented to accomplish objectives.

Symptom—An observable fact in the environment that may be used to diagnose a problem.

Synergy—The phenomenon by which the combined output is greater than the sum of its parts.

Team—A group of individuals united by a common mission.

Training—Imparting knowledge and skills required for performance.

Trait leadership—A theory of leadership that suggests that the characteristics of an individual determine the ability to lead others.

Transactional leadership—A theory of leadership that focuses on the interactions of the leader and followers to determine leadership effectiveness.

Transformation process—A process that converts resources (inputs) into products and services (outputs).

Transformational leadership—A theory of leadership that considers value systems of followers, leaders, and organizations as components of the leadership process.

Two-factor theory—A content theory of motivation that defines external needs as hygiene factors and internal needs as motivators.

Value-added supervision—Supervisory practices that enhance productivity.

WIFM—An acronym that stands for "What's in it for me"; used to describe the awareness of motivational factors for training and leadership.

Work Life Development Model—A model that depicts the developmental life cycle of an individual from the introduction to full-time work through retirement from full-time work.

Index

(Page numbers in italic indicate illustrations.)